This book is dedicated to the memory of Pat Berry

Preface

This book is intended as a starting point both for those called upon to advise partnerships and for those considering the partnership vehicle themselves. Read as a whole, it provides a comprehensive overview of both law and practice, whilst it can also be dipped into by those requiring quick, clear and simple information and advice on any element of the subject. It may act as a refresher for those who are unfamiliar with the topic, and as a springboard for further investigation using the practical advice, contact addresses and suggestions for further reading given. Since the book appears at a time when, having for so long remained relatively static, partnership law is entering a period of fundamental change, we include guidance as to the potential changes.

The authors wish to thank all those who have assisted in the preparation of the book, in particular, John Snape for his comments on the chapter on taxation, and Adrian Walters for his comments on the sample partnership agreement. Any errors or omission remain, of course, ours alone.

Elspeth Deards and Russell Deards
August 1999

Contents

1 What is a Partnership?

1.1 The legal definition

The legal definition of what constitutes a partnership is provided by s 1(1) of the Partnership Act 1890 (the 1890 Act) (Appendix 1), which defines it as 'the relation which subsists between persons carrying on a business in common with a view of profit'. Therefore, if persons have agreed to form a partnership, they will be regarded as a partnership in the eyes of the law only if they comply with the requirements of s 1(1) of the 1890 Act. If the arrangement is informal, and the parties have not actually thought about forming a partnership, it is still possible that the law will regard them as partners. This is because any entity that satisfies the definition in s 1(1) will automatically be a partnership, whether this is intended or not. It is therefore important to understand the legal definition when advising those considering setting up a partnership, and also when advising on the possible rights and obligations of those who have undertaken a joint business venture and who might fulfil the definition of a partnership without intending to. (An example of the latter situation is provided by *Spicer (Keith) Ltd v Mansell* [1970] 1 All ER 462: see 1.1.3.)

What are the requirements of the legal definition?

1.1.1 Relation

As this word implies, a partnership is not an entity in its own right, like a company, but a relationship based on a contract between two or more people. A partnership does not have a legal personality separate to that of the partners, and therefore cannot make contracts or own land (see 2.3, 3.4.3 and 5.1). The relation between members of a company is expressly excluded from the definition by s 1(2)(a) of the 1890 Act, and therefore a company cannot be a partnership, although it can be a partner (see 1.1.2).

1.1.2 Between persons

Natural persons (individuals) may be partners and, since companies are regarded as persons by the law, they can also be partners.

1.1.3 Carrying on business

Section 45 of the 1890 Act defines a business as including 'every trade occupation, or profession'. More difficult than the question of whether there is a business is the question of whether that business is being carried on. That is to say, has the business progressed from the initial stages of being set up to such a stage that it can be said to be being carried on? If it has not yet progressed to this stage, it has not become a partnership.

For example, in *Spicer (Keith) Ltd v Mansell* (see 1.1), Mansell and Bishop planned to set up a company to run a restaurant. Before the company was formed, Bishop ordered goods from Spicer Ltd for the business and a joint bank account was opened. Bishop then became bankrupt, which meant that Spicer Ltd was unlikely to be paid by him personally. Spicer Ltd therefore decided to sue Mansell on the basis that he and Bishop had been partners. The court held that there was no partnership, since the parties had not yet reached the stage of carrying on business together, but had only been preparing to do so. Ordering goods and opening a joint bank account was not enough.

Similarly, in *Khan v Miah* [1998] 1 WLR 477, four individuals agreed to go into partnership together to run a restaurant. They entered into various contracts with third parties, and one of them leased premises. Three of them took out a bank loan and two of them opened a joint bank account and informed the bank that they were partners for the purposes of the account. The restaurant was never opened, and the question arose as to whether a partnership existed. The Court of Appeal held that no partnership existed because no business had been carried on. All the activities had been preparatory to the carrying on of a business. (Note that leave has been given in this case for an appeal to the House of Lords and a hearing is not expected to be listed until late 1999 at the earliest.)

1.1.4 In common

This means that the partners participate in the business, which effectively means that they have the right to manage it. Section 24(5) of the 1890

Act provides that every partner must have a say in management (see 4.3). This can be altered by agreement, but since all partners are liable for debts and obligations of the partnership, it is understandable that they will normally want to be involved in management, or at least be kept fully informed of all decisions in a timely fashion.

Whether the requirement of carrying on a business 'in common' is satisfied by a particular business depends on the facts of the case. It will not be satisfied by, for example, a relationship with a supplier, since although a supplier carries on business with the partnership it has no right to be involved in management.

1.1.5 With a view of profit

The key to this element of the definition is that the parties must intend to make a profit. It is not necessary that a profit is actually made; a business which ceases before profits are made could still be a partnership during its brief life. For example, in finding that no partnership existed in *Khan v Miah* (see 1.1.3) because the business had never actually been carried on, the court noted that it was not essential for there to have been any profits or actual monies received, since the carrying on of a business need only be 'with a view of profit'.

1.2 Guidelines under s 2

Section 2 of the 1890 Act provides further assistance in assessing whether there is a partnership. It does not give hard and fast rules, but simply states that the existence of certain facts will be prima facie evidence of a partnership (that is to say, they can indicate that there may be a partnership, but in practice the court will look at all the evidence) and that the existence of certain other facts does not, of itself, create a partnership.

Section 2(1) provides that joint ownership of property does not of itself create a partnership. So, if A and B own a house, this alone will not create a partnership between them. However, if in addition they rent it out as a business, they could be in partnership.

Section 2(2) provides that sharing gross returns is not sufficient to prove the existence of a partnership, but that sharing net profits (turnover (all the money used in the business) less outgoings (rent, salaries, stock, etc)) will be prima facie evidence. In *Cox v Coulson* [1916] 2 KB 177, the court held that the sharing of gross box office receipts by two parties to a theatrical venture was not sufficient to evidence the existence of a partnership.

Section 2(3) of the 1890 Act provides that sharing profits is prima facie evidence of partnership, but that there are a number of exceptions to this:

- partners can pay off a creditor by instalments out of profits without the creditor becoming a partner (*Cox v Hickman* (1860) 8 HL Cas 268);

- partners can pay employees or agents by way of a share of profits. This allows the partnership to run a profit sharing or bonus scheme for employees without those employees becoming partners;

- partners can pay an annuity out of profits to a widow or child of a deceased partner;

- partners can pay interest on a loan made to the partnership by a share of net profits. If the lender is paid a fixed rate of interest then there is clearly no question of their being a partner, but where they take a share of the profits, it would risk becoming a partner if it was not for this provision. However, s 2(3)(d) provides that this exception will only apply if the contract of loan is in writing and is signed by all the parties. In addition, lenders must take care that the contract does not give them rights akin to those of partners. In *Pooley v Driver* (1877) 5 Ch 458, an agreement between partners and lenders provided that: the lenders had the right to ensure that the business was being properly run; that the interest repayable varied not only according to profits, but also according to the proportion which the loan bore to the capital; and that the lenders were entitled to share in any surplus profits on dissolution and must return interest paid if losses had been made. This was held to be a partnership agreement. As a result, the lenders were partners;

- if partners purchase another business, they can pay for the goodwill in it by a share of profits. This has the advantage that they need not find all the money to pay for the business at the time of sale. In effect, it is a device to aid cash flow.

1.3 Key features of a partnership and the 1890 Act

1.3.1 Flexibility

As discussed in 1.1, a partnership may arise without any formal agreement by the partners, and indeed can arise without their even being aware that this is so. To the extent that there is no contrary agreement, they are governed by the 1890 Act which runs to only 50 sections. Relatively few other statutes apply to partnerships. In addition, a partnership need not be registered nor need it file accounts, and is thus a more flexible and informal way of being in business with others than a company (see Chapter 2).

1.3.2 Personal liability

The other key feature of a partnership is the personal liability of the partners. Partners have unlimited liability, which means that, if the assets of the partnership are insufficient to meet its liabilities, the partners' personal assets are available to creditors of the partnership. Thus, partners stand to lose not only the investment which they decided to make in the partnership (which is a risk run by most investors), but also the assets which they did not choose to invest.

1.3.3 Joint and several liability

The significance of personal liability is increased by the fact that liability is also joint and several. Section 9 of the 1890 Act provides that partners are jointly liable for debts of the partnership, while s 3 of the Civil Liability (Contributions) Act 1978 effectively imposes several liability for such debts. Section 12 of the 1890 Act provides that partners are also jointly and severally liable for wrongful acts or omissions or the misapplication of property.

This means that each partner is liable for the acts of the other partners (joint liability) and that a creditor may sue any combination of partners or a single partner, such action being of itself no bar to further action against other partners (several liability). Where only some of the partners are sued, they can insist on the other partners being made parties if they are within the jurisdiction and can be found (*Robinson v Geisel* [1894] 2 QB 685: see 12.2).

1.4   Types of partnerships

1.4.1   General partnerships

The 1890 Act applies only to general partnerships in which all partners are general partners, that is to say, they have the liability discussed in 1.3.2 and these partnerships may further be classified as follows.

Trading partnerships

In *Wheatley v Smithers* [1906] 2 KB 321, the court defined a trading partnership as one requiring the buying and selling of goods.

Non-trading partnerships

These are partnerships which do not come within the definition of trading partnerships. They include professional partnerships, that is to say, partnerships where all or most partners are members of professions, such as accountancy (see further Chapter 10). These partnerships have special rules as to the number of partners (see 1.5).

1.4.2   Limited partnerships

The Limited Partnerships Act 1907 (Appendix 2) provides that partners may form limited partnerships (which must be registered) in which one or more partners have limited liability, so long as at least one partner has unlimited liability. However, as s 6 provides that limited partners may not take part in management and have no authority to bind the firm, this form of partnership is unsuitable for most businesses. If a limited partner does take part in management, s 6 provides that they become liable for all debts of the partnership incurred while they do so.

Section 7 of the Limited Partnerships Act provides that, subject to its provisions, the 1890 Act and all relevant case law apply to limited partnerships. This book will therefore only deal separately with the law relating to limited partnerships where that law diverges from the law applicable to general partnerships.

1.5   Number of partners

Section 716 of the Companies Act 1985 provides for a maximum of 20 partners for most partnerships, but solicitors and accountants are expressly excepted. In addition, a number of statutory instruments provide exemptions from this maximum number for other professions, including estate agents, auctioneers, architects and surveyors.

1.6   Types of partners

Although the law recognises only general partners (and limited partners in the context of limited partnerships), in practice there may be other versions of a 'partner'. For example:

*   partners who retire but who leave their capital in the partnership are often described as 'sleeping' or 'dormant' partners. As far as the law is concerned, they continue to be partners if they do not give proper notice of their retirement to third parties or are held out to third parties as partners (see 5.4.2 and 5.5);

*   the word 'partner' is also commonly used to describe a salaried partner who does not receive a share of profits but a salary. In practice, this is often used as a form of promotion for employees prior to making them full partners. As with dormant partners, as far as the law is concerned, salaried partners will be liable as partners if they are held out as partners and reliance is placed on that fact (see 5.5).

It may well be that, in both these cases, the 'partner' has no management rights and is not regarded as a partner by the other partners. However, an internal agreement of the partners cannot affect the liability of the partnership to third parties to whom the dormant or salaried partner appears to be a general partner. It is therefore advisable for the 'partner' in question to obtain an indemnity from the partners against any claim made by a creditor on the basis of his apparent status as a partner. Such an indemnity is, of course, only as good as the partners who gave it (see 5.4.2). In addition to the risks run by these 'partners', their existence can also cause problems to the partnership itself, since it may be liable for their acts (see 5.5).

1.7   Duration of partnership

1.7.1 Partnership 'at will'

Section 26(1) of the 1890 Act provides that if no agreement as to duration has been reached the partnership is 'at will'. This means that it continues indefinitely and that any partner may dissolve the partnership by giving notice to all other partners. Section 26(2) of the 1890 Act provides that if the partnership was originally constituted by deed (not just by agreement in writing: see 3.1) the notice must be in writing. This can take effect as soon as all partners are notified, although the partner giving notice may specify a future date. This means that any partner can dissolve the partnership almost instantly at any time. For practical reasons it is, therefore, advisable to provide in the partnership agreement for a minimum notice period, for example, of three or six months, to allow the other partners to formulate a plan for breaking up the business or forming a new partnership and paying off the partner who leaves (see 5.4.2.1).

1.7.2 Fixed term or purpose

Instead of having a partnership at will, the partners may agree that the partnership should continue for a particular period of time or purpose, with or without provisions to apply in the event that the partners wish to continue the partnership afterwards. A common provision is that the partnership will continue until the partners unanimously agree otherwise. Such a partnership will dissolve automatically at the end of the specified period or purpose unless the partnership is, in fact, continued. If this is the case, the partnership will be governed by the old terms unless new terms are agreed (s 27 of the 1890 Act). If no new agreement as to duration is reached, it will be a partnership at will.

1.7.3 Other events

Certain other events, such as the death or bankruptcy of a partner, will automatically dissolve the partnership unless there is contrary agreement. This is discussed in more detail in Chapter 8. In addition, in certain circumstances a partnership may be dissolved by the court (see 8.1.2).

1.8 Practical advice

One difficulty with this area of law is that clients often fail to seek advice at the outset. This may mean that they have formed a partnership without realising it or at least without being aware of the legal consequences. It is therefore essential to address with all clients engaged or planning to engage in some joint business relationship the issue of whether there is or will be a partnership and to advise on an appropriate partnership agreement if necessary (see 3.1). Where a client does seek advice prior to forming a partnership, advice should also be given as to alternative business entities. This issue will be considered in Chapter 2.

2 Partnerships and Other Forms of Business Medium Compared

The chief rival to a partnership as a business medium is the private limited company. As stated in 1.3.1, the key advantages of a partnership are its flexibility and informality. A company can, however, be advantageous because of its limited liability status and the protection this offers to its directors and shareholders in ordinary circumstances. In addition, it is possible to use a limited partnership as a business medium (see 1.4.2 and 3.5) or a joint venture not involving the formation of a partnership or a company (see 2.9).

If a client seeks legal advice on the most attractive vehicle for a commercial venture, the matters outlined in this chapter should always be considered.

2.1 Flexibility and informality

Partnerships are more flexible and informal than companies because of the contractual relationship which is at their heart. For example, partners enjoy flexibility with regard to the size of their respective shares and drawings and as to their roles within the partnership in response to changing business needs. Partnerships are not required to register or even to have an agreement, although an agreement is clearly advisable (see 3.1). No documents have to be filed and there is no annual audit. By contrast, companies must register certain information on registration (see 2.2) and are under a continuing duty to notify the Registrar of Companies of any changes to this information. They must be audited annually and file an annual return. Directors of companies have greater duties in respect of transactions with their own business and other benefits than partners do.

2.2   Setting up the business

It is possible to set up a partnership more easily than a company because no formalities need be completed by a partnership. The formation and terms of a partnership may be evidenced by a partnership deed, by a written agreement, or simply an oral agreement, and there are no legal requirements as to the content of any agreement. The process of setting up a partnership may, however, take longer if the partnership decides to draw up a written partnership agreement or partnership deed (see 3.1).

By contrast, a company may not commence business until it has received a certificate of incorporation from the Registrar of Companies. This may only be obtained on registration of a Memorandum of Articles (setting out basic information about the company), Articles of Association (containing detailed information about how the company will be run), Form 10 (stating the first directors and company secretary), Form 12 (statutory declaration of compliance with the Companies Act 1985) and the fee (currently £20). The documents should be sent to the Registrar at the Companies House in the part of the United Kingdom in which the company is to have its registered office (as set out in the table below).

It is, however, possible to speed up the process of incorporation by, for example, paying a higher fee for same day incorporation (currently £100), adopting Table A to the Companies Act 1985 as the company's articles in whole or in part (instead of drafting a tailor made set of articles from scratch) or buying a ready made company 'off the shelf' from a company agent or solicitor. This can be done at the same branch of Companies House as ordinary registration or at one of the other branches (as set out in the table below). (Contact details for Companies House are provided in Chapter 16.)

Registered office in	Register at Companies House in	Same day incorporation at Companies House in
England or Wales	Cardiff	Cardiff, Birmingham, Leeds, London, or Manchester
Scotland	Edinburgh	Edinburgh or Glasgow
Northern Ireland	Belfast	Belfast

2.3   Separate legal personality

A partnership has no legal personality separate to that of its partners, whereas a company is regarded by the law as a separate legal person to its shareholders and directors (known as the rule in *Salomon v Salomon* after the case of *Salomon v A Salomon & Co Ltd* [1897] AC 22). This enables a number of advantages, which are denied to partnerships, to be conferred upon a company:

• a company may own its own property, including land;
• a company may enter into, enforce, and be liable on contracts;
• shares in a company are freely transferable;
• a company has perpetual succession, that is to say, it continues in existence regardless of changes in its shareholders.

However, it should be noted that the law does recognise the partnership entity for some purposes. For example, it can sue and be sued (Civil Procedure Rules (CPR) Scheds 1 and 2, applying the Rules of the Supreme Court (RSC) Ord 81 and the County Court Rules Ord 5 r 1); it is recognised for VAT purposes (s 45 of the Value Added Tax Act 1994); if insolvent, it may be wound up as if it was an unregistered company; and execution against partnership property is possible if judgment is obtained against the firm (see 12.5).

2.4   Liability

The liability of shareholders in a company is limited to the amount which they have invested in shares. If the company becomes insolvent, neither the shareholders nor the directors are liable to contribute from their personal assets. As discussed in 1.3.2 and 5.3, partners have unlimited liability and must contribute to the partnership's assets from their personal assets if the partnership is insolvent.

There are, however, instances in which the 'corporate veil' will be pierced and the directors or the shareholders treated as one and the same as the company. This means that they can be made personally liable for the company's debts and obligations. These instances are known as exceptions to the rule in *Salomon v Salomon* (see 2.3) and include the following:

• where the veil of incorporation is being used for fraudulent purposes. For example, in *Gilford Motor Co Ltd v Horne* [1933] All ER 109, Horne was subject to covenants in favour of his former employer that he would not solicit their clients or engage in a competing business. He set up a company, with his wife and another ex-employee of his former employer as the directors and shareholders, through which he solicited clients. Horne claimed that he was not in breach of his covenants, since it was the company which was poaching clients, and the company was a separate legal person. The court held that the veil should be pierced on account of the fraud and that the position in reality was that the company and Horne were one and the same person;

- ss 213–14 of the Insolvency Act 1986 provide that directors and other officers of the company may be liable to contribute to its assets in the event of insolvency if they have acted to defraud creditors or have continued to trade when it was clear that the company could not survive, thus increasing the losses (see 9.3.5);

- s 349 of the Companies Act 1985 provides that, if an officer (defined as a director, manager or company secretary) of the company signs on behalf of the company without mentioning the company's name, that officer will then be personally liable on that document if it is not honoured by the company.

In practice, directors of small companies may also be asked to give personal guarantees for the company's performance to lenders, which effectively impose personal liability on them.

2.5 Control

Partners retain personal control because they both own the business and manage its affairs on a day to day basis. In companies, shareholders do not automatically have personal control since it is the directors who manage the business. This has the advantage that it can reduce the risk of poor management resulting from management responsibilities being held on the basis of financial investment, rather than expertise. However, in small companies, it is common for the same people to be shareholders and directors, while in larger partnerships the concept of control by the partners is less meaningful, since it is not practicable for large numbers of partners to actually take part in management on a regular basis. Indeed, it might be undesirable, since it is unlikely that all partners will have the necessary management skills.

2.6 Finance

Partnerships are generally more restricted than companies in their ability to raise finance, both internally and externally.

2.6.1 Internal finance

Although partners contribute capital just as shareholders invest in shares, most partnerships are subject to a maximum of 20 partners (see 1.5), whereas there is no statutory limit on the number of shareholders (although private companies may impose a limit if they wish, and may not, in any case, offer shares to the public). Secondly, shareholders are by definition those who can and wish to invest money in a business. Partners, on the other hand, may be interested primarily in managing or working for the business, and may have little ability or desire to invest in the business. Thirdly, investment in a partnership may be less attractive than in a company, since it carries with it the risks of unlimited liability (see 1.3.2) and the right to manage (see 1.1.4 and 4.3). Although the latter need not be exercised, for most partners the status of a partner represents both an investment and a job, and this is clearly unsuitable for some potential investors.

2.6.2 External finance

Both partnerships and companies may be able to borrow from banks or other bodies on the security of a fixed charge. This is a charge which is regarded as 'fixed' to certain assets and the business may not dispose of those assets without the permission of the lender. It is therefore only appropriate for assets, such as land, which the business does not need to dispose of frequently. However, companies have the advantage of being able to offer lenders the additional security of a floating charge. This is a charge which is regarded as 'floating' over assets, and is therefore suitable also for assets in which the company deals on a day to day basis, such as stock in trade and cash at bank. Companies may therefore be able to raise more money in this way.

2.7 Taxation

The rates and rules of taxation are different for companies and partnerships (see further Chapter 11 on the taxation of partnerships). The rates of taxation are often higher for partnership profits (if the partners are liable to higher rate income tax) than for company profits (corporation tax). However, the profits of the partnership are taxed only once (in the hands of the partners), whereas those of the company are taxed twice (when made by the company and then when distributed to shareholders in the form of dividends or to directors in the form of salaries). The most advantageous business status for tax purposes will therefore depend on the finances of a particular business. This is an area where specialist advice is needed.

2.8   Publicly available information

Since partnerships are not required to register information about themselves, public access to information about them is limited to the partners' names (see 3.3) unless all partners with unlimited liability are themselves limited companies. If this is the case, the accounts must be publicly available. In contrast, the information which companies must, by law, provide to the Registrar of Companies (including accounts) is available for public inspection at any branch of Companies House (for details, see Chapter 16).

Credit reference agencies can also provide information about a business in return for a fee. However, they will usually have financial information only about the individual partners' assets and not the partnership assets. They are likely to have much more information about the financial standing of a company.

2.9   Joint ventures

Joint ventures are another vehicle for combining the skills and resources of two or more people or companies in order to achieve a common business objective. Each of the parties remains a separate legal entity, but enters into an agreement for the purpose of a particular project. A joint venture agreement should set out clearly the ambit of each party's role and liability. Joint ventures are common in the oil and gas, construction and property sectors and are used in many 'collaboration agreements' between companies or companies and other bodies.

Care should always be taken to ensure that the joint venture does not satisfy the legal definition of a partnership (see 1.1) unless that is what is intended. It is perhaps difficult to imagine a joint venture which does not involve the establishment of a joint venture company and yet does not satisfy the definition of a partnership. However, it could include a joint venture with a partnership (since that is not a 'person') or a joint venture which carries out activities which are not intended to make a profit (such as research or training).

Some joint ventures could be viewed by the courts as unincorporated associations. There is no completely satisfactory legal definition of an unincorporated association but, broadly speaking, it is a non-profit making association of persons (natural or legal) which exists for the mutual benefit of its members, which has not been incorporated, and which is not a partnership. The concept typically includes unincorporated clubs and societies. Most commercial joint ventures are, it seems, not capable of being categorised as unincorporated associations within the present (unclear) definition of an unincorporated association, because of the intention to make a profit. The area of joint ventures is one in which more specialist texts should be consulted.

2.10 Table of advantages and disadvantages

PARTNERSHIPS		COMPANIES	
Advantages	Disadvantages	Advantages	Disadvantages
Flexible and informal.			Lacks flexibility and informality.
Quick and easy to set up (but less so if a proper agreement is drawn up).			Requires statutory documents to be drawn up and registered prior to trading.
	Lacks separate legal personality and therefore cannot own land or contract in their own name, shares in them are not freely transferable and they lack perpetual succession.	Have separate legal personality, with its associated advantages.	
	Partners have unlimited liability for the business's debts and wrongful acts.	Shareholders have limited liability (but, if also directors, may be asked to give personal guarantees, and may be liable if the corporate veil is pierced).	
Partners control the business (but the majority investor is not entitled, without further agreement, to any greater degree of control than any other partner).			Shareholders have little control over the business (but a majority shareholder has considerably more power than the others).
	Limited in terms of raising finance.	A wider range of finance options are available, particularly to public companies.	
No information is publicly available, with the exception of the partners' names.			Information concerning the business is publicly available.

Taxation is not listed in this table because, as discussed at 2.7, whether a partnership or a company is more advantageous in terms of taxation depends entirely on the nature of the business and its finances.

2.11 Practical advice

In summary, the main options for setting up in business with other people or entities are as follows:

- a **partnership**. Each partner has joint and several liability and this liability is unlimited. Third parties may therefore issue proceedings against just one partner, who is obliged to meet all the liabilities of the partnership (see 12.2), although he may be entitled to seek a contribution from the other partners (see 5.4.2);

- a **limited partnership**. This is similar to a partnership, but whilst there must be a least one general partner with unlimited liability, the others may be limited partners and limit their liability to the extent of their capital contribution (see 1.4.2 and 3.5);

- a **company**. This has the advantage that shareholders' liability is limited to the amount which they have agree to invest in shares, although this is subject to any personal guarantees which shareholders who are also directors may have been required to give by the company's bank. In addition, in the long term, continuity can more easily be maintained with a company. The comparative advantages and disadvantages of companies and partnerships are summarised in 2.10;

- a **joint venture** not involving a company or partnership (see 2.9).

When advising clients, always bear in mind the advantages and disadvantages of a partnership over other forms of business medium, and clearly explain the options to the clients. Most importantly, seek to accommodate the client's needs with the appropriate medium for them and also consider whether some form of joint venture not involving a partnership or company might be appropriate.

If the client requires additional advice which the adviser does not feel qualified to give, for example, on taxation considerations, they should explain that to the client and, if they are able, recommend the appropriate person to give that advice. If they do not do this, the client may be entitled to view them as a 'general adviser' and, if problems arise later, may claim that their silence on a particular area in effect amounted to advice that it was not an important or relevant consideration (*Hurlingham Estates v Wilde and Partners* [1997] STC 627: see 11.6).

3 Setting up a Partnership

3.1 The partnership agreement

There is no legal obligation to have a partnership agreement or to have any such agreement in writing. However, it is advisable both to have an agreement and to put it in writing for two reasons. First, it promotes certainty by allowing the partners to set out their respective rights and liabilities, anticipate problems and agree a mechanism for resolving disputes. Secondly, an agreement (whether in writing or not) is the only way in which the provisions of the 1890 Act can be disapplied.

Like other contracts, a partnership agreement will be construed in the light of the parties' objectives. For example, in *Hitchman v Crouch Butler Savage Associates* (1983) 127 SJ 441, a requirement in the agreement that all expulsion notices be signed by a particular partner was held by the court not to apply when that partner was himself expelled. Terms may also be implied by the court to give the partnership agreement business efficacy (*Miles v Clarke* [1953] 1 All ER 779: see 3.4).

The following clauses should be included (or at least considered) in any agreement.

- preliminary clauses (parties, date of commencement, nature of business, name and place of business);
- duration;
- management and decision making (including meetings and restrictions on authority);
- duties, including utmost good faith;
- time devoted to business, holidays and absence;
- restrictions on the activities of partners while they are partners and afterwards;

- indemnity of other partners against private debts;
- profits and losses;
- drawings;
- keeping of books, right of access by partners and return of documents on retirement;
- dispute resolution during the currency of the agreement and upon dissolution;
- retirement;
- expulsion;
- option to purchase share of outgoing partner;
- capital (including any provision for interest and for further capital contributions to be made as agreed);
- property;
- insurance;
- definition of goodwill;
- bank details, requirements for all funds to be paid in, cheque signing;
- appointment of accountants, year end date;
- procedure for amending the agreement;
- dissolution (including buy out provisions);
- winding up and insolvency procedures.

An example of a partnership agreement is included in Appendix 4. It is set out in the form of a deed simply because this is common practice for partnership agreements. There is, however, no legal requirement that the agreement take the form of a deed, and an ordinary agreement will suffice. As always, when taking instructions from clients it is important not merely to advise on the basis of such a checklist, but to seek specific instructions and advise upon them.

3.2   Amending the agreement

Any agreement reached may be amended subsequently. The agreement itself may provide a procedure for amendment or, if it does not, s 19 of the 1890 Act provides that the agreement may be varied by consent of all partners. This consent may be express or implied from a course of dealings. For example, in *Pilling v Pilling* (1865) 3 De GJ & Sm 162; 46 ER 599, the partnership agreement gave complex provisions about the allocation of profits and interest on capital. The partnership lasted 11 years during which time the agreement was ignored and money allocated differently. The court held that the agreement had been validly altered.

It must be remembered that s 19, like other provisions of the 1890 Act which apply to the internal running of the partnership, only applies in the absence of contrary agreement. Therefore, if a partnership agreement has an express provision stating that any amendment must be in writing, this would effectively disapply s 19 of the 1890 Act and the agreement could not be altered by a course of dealing.

3.3   The name of the partnership

The name may consist of the surnames (with initials or forenames) of all individual partners, and the corporate names of all corporate partners, with an indication of succession to a former business (for example, 'Smith and Smith (formerly Smith and Bloggs)') if desired. Such a name is permitted even if there is another firm with a similar name, unless it is part of a scheme to deceive the public. In *Croft v Day* (1843) 7 Beav 84; 49 ER 994, partners by the names of Day and Martin set up a partnership to manufacture blacking, and adopted the Day and Martin name for the fraudulent purpose of representing to the public that they were the (then) well known blacking manufacturer of that name. The fraud was further evidenced by the fact that the partnership used containers which resembled those used by the original firm. The court granted an injunction to prevent the use of the Day and Martin name by the partnership.

Anything other than such a name must comply with the Business Names Act 1985, which has two limbs: restrictions on the name which may be used; and requirements for the disclosure of partners' names,

3.3.1 Restrictions on name

Section 2 of the Business Names Act provides that approval of the Secretary of State for Trade and Industry is required in order to trade under certain names:

* a name which suggests a connection with central or local government (because people would assume the business is officially regulated and has financial backing); or

* a name which contains a word listed in the Companies and Business Names Regulations 1981 as amended. These are names which imply something specific about the business, such as 'international' or 'insurance'. This means that there is a check that the business really is, for example, international or involves insurance.

In the case of some words listed in the Regulations, the approval of another body may also be required for a name incorporating that word. The Regulations specify which body must give approval, for example, the Charity Commissioners or the Scottish Home and Health Department (as well as the Secretary of State for Trade and Industry) must approve the use of the words 'charity' or 'charitable'.

Professional bodies, such as The Law Society, may also impose restrictions on the names used by their members.

3.3.2 Disclosure

Section 4 of the Business Names Act provides that the name of all partners and an address where they can be served with official documents (usually the firm's address) must be displayed at the firm's premises and on the following documents:

- business letters;

- written orders for goods or services to be supplied to the business;

- invoices and receipts issued in the course of the business;

- written demands for payment of debts arising in the course of business.

It is not clear whether e-mails are also required to contain this information, but it is the view of The Law Society (so far as solicitors are concerned) that they are not ((1998) Law Society's Gazette 38, p 39).

If there are more than 20 partners, it may instead be stated on letters and documents that a list of partners and an address for service is displayed at the principal place of business.

3.3.3 Sanctions

Failure to disclose this information is both a criminal offence, which renders the partners liable to a fine, and a civil wrong. This means that contracts made by the partnership while it is in breach of the Business Names Act are unenforceable if the other party can prove that he was unable to pursue a claim against the partnership because of the breach, or that he has suffered loss as a result of the breach.

In addition, if the name is similar to that of a competitor so as to deceive or cause confusion, its use may expose the partners to the risk of liability under the tort of passing off. This tort consists of the following (per Lord Diplock in *Erven Warnink BV v Townend & Sons (Hull) Ltd* [1979] 2 All ER 927, pp 932–33):

- a misrepresentation;
- made by a trader in the course of business;
- to a prospective or ultimate consumer of the goods or services supplied by him;
- which is calculated to damage the business or goodwill of another trader;
- which causes such damage.

However, where the public is not actually confused or deceived by the misrepresentation, it will not constitute passing off (*Cadbury-Schweppes Pty Ltd v Pub Squash Co Pty Ltd* [1981] 1 All ER 213).

3.4   Partnership property

Section 20 of the 1890 Act defines partnership property as:

> All property and rights and interests in property originally brought into the partnership stock or acquired, whether by purchase or otherwise, on account of the firm, or for the purposes and in the course of the partnership business.

The reference to property brought into the partnership stock will cover property brought in as capital by a partner, and s 21 of the 1890 Act provides that property bought with the partnership's money is presumed to have been bought for the partnership. Property itemised in the partnership's accounts will also be regarded as partnership property.

In the absence of agreement by the partners, mere use of property by the partnership is generally insufficient for it to be regarded as partnership property. However, an example of a case where mere use was held to be enough was *Waterer v Waterer* (1872–73) 15 LR Eq 402, where land used in a nursery business was held to be partnership property because of the nature of the business (the land could not be separated from the trees and shrubs growing in it which were stock in trade).

In *Miles v Clarke* [1953] 1 All ER 779, which concerned a photography business, the court held that only property which was necessary to give business efficacy to the relationship constituted partnership property. The stocks of film used in the course of the business were therefore partnership property, but the negatives and prints brought in to the business, and the lease of the premises, were not. They continued to belong to the partners who brought them in.

Section 20 of the 1890 Act also includes property to which a partner is entitled and which all partners have agreed should be partnership property, regardless of whether it can be assigned by that partner. In *Don King Productions Inc v Warren and Others* [1999] 2 All ER 218, partners agreed to assign to the firm personal contracts which contained provisions against assignment. The court ruled that the agreement to assign should be construed as a declaration of trust by each partner and was enforceable by the firm.

Since the definition of partnership property in s 20 of the 1890 Act is not as clear as it might be, and the consequences of property being partnership property are significant (see 3.4.1–3.4.4), it is advisable to define or identify in the agreement what belongs to the partnership (as opposed to individual partners).

If property is partnership property, whether by virtue of s 20 of the 1890 Act or a partnership agreement, certain consequences follow. The most important are set out in 3.4.1–3.4.4.

3.4.1 Creditors' claims

If the property belongs to the partnership, then creditors of the partnership have first claim on it and only after their claims are satisfied may the private creditors of an insolvent partner claim on his share of partnership property. However, if the property belongs to the partnership, then in the event that the partnership's assets are insufficient to meet the claims of partnership creditors, those creditors rank equally with the partner's private creditors in claiming against his individual property. (See the Insolvent Partnerships Order 1994, discussed in Chapter 9). Thus, the distinction between partnership property and property of a partner is of great importance to the creditors if the partnership (or a partner) is insolvent.

Section 23 of the 1890 Act provides that a private judgment creditor (that is to say, a creditor who has obtained judgment in court that he is owed money) of a partner in a private capacity cannot pay himself out of the assets of the firm. He must apply to the court for an order charging the partner's share. The other partners can redeem the share by paying off the creditor and they can then claim the cost of this back from the partner (if the partner has sufficient assets).

In order to protect the partnership, it may be advisable to provide for the expulsion from the partnership of a partner against whom such judgment has been obtained (see further 7.4). If this is accompanied by the paying off of the partner's share, this will prevent the judgment creditor charging the assets of the partnership, since the former partner no longer owns a share of them.

3.4.2 Dealing with the property

If property belongs to a partner, he can do as he likes with it, unless the partnership has a contract to use it. However, if it is partnership property, s 20 of the 1890 Act provides that it 'must be held and applied by the partners exclusively for the purposes of the partnership and in accordance with the partnership agreement'. This, of course, is subject to contrary agreement.

3.4.3 Nature of ownership

Partnership property is held by the partners on trust for each other (*Fawcett v Whitehouse* (1829) 1 Russ & M 132; 39 ER 51; *Clegg v Fishwick* (1849) 1 Mac & G 294; 41 ER 1278). Where the property in question is land, the partners hold the land on trust for themselves with a maximum of four as trustees (s 34 of the Law of Property Act 1925).

3.4.4 Accounting for the property

If the value of partnership property increases or decreases, that is an asset or a liability of the partnership and is recorded in its accounts, whereas, if the property belongs to a partner, the appreciation or depreciation also belongs to him.

It should be noted that, in the absence of contrary agreement, partnership property is to be valued at its current market value for the purposes of ascertaining the value of a partner's share on retirement or dissolution. This is so even if the normal accounting practice of the firm is to value it at cost (*Re White (Deceased), White v Minnis and Another* [1999] 2 All ER 663).

3.4.5 Valuing the property

There is no single standard way of assessing the value of partnership property. The partners may agree to value it at cost, at market price, or at cost plus a set figure for appreciation or depreciation (depending on the nature of the asset). The valuation of an asset may have tax consequences (see Chapter 11) and will certainly be relevant if the partnership business is sold or a partner disposes of his share in the partnership (see 8.3).

SETTING UP A PARTNERSHIP   25

3.4.6 Goodwill

The 1890 Act makes no reference to goodwill (defined in *Trego v Hunt* [1896] AC 7 as 'the whole advantage, whatever it may be, of the reputation of the firm, which may have been built up by years of honest work or gained by lavish expenditure of money', per Lord Macnaghten, p 24). It is therefore advisable to include in the partnership agreement either a method for calculating goodwill or a statement that it is to have a nominal or nil value (see *Deacons v Bridge* [1984] 2 All ER 19). The latter has the advantage of reducing the cost of a partner's share to a new partner, and thus may be particularly appropriate for a family business where the partners want the next generation to be able to afford to buy shares in the partnership. Such an approach may also have tax consequences (see Chapter 11).

Possible alternatives for the calculation of goodwill include the following:

• the net profit basis. This means that goodwill is valued by reference to the average net profits over a specified number of years and multiplied by a specified figure, such as two;

• the gross receipts basis. This means that goodwill is valued by reference to a specified proportion (for example, one-half) of the average gross fees of the partnership over a specified number of years;

• the excess profits basis. This means that goodwill is valued by reference to the profits which the partner whose share is to be valued could have earned elsewhere, less the average profits of the partnership over a specified number of years;

• the book value basis. This means that goodwill is valued as it has been in the partnership accounts.

3.5   Limited partnerships

As mentioned in 1.4.2, the setting up of a limited partnership requires that it be registered with the Registrar at Companies House in that part of the United Kingdom in which the principal place of business is situated or is to be situated (see below).

Registration requires the submission of a fee (currently £2) payable to Companies House and Form LP5 (see Appendix 3) containing the following information:

• the firm's name;

• the general nature of the business;

- the address of the principal place of business;
- the full name of each of the partners, listing general and limited partners separately;
- the term (if any) for which the partnership is entered into;
- the date of its commencement;
- a statement that the partnership is limited and the description of every partner as such;
- the sum contributed by each limited partner, and whether it is paid in cash or otherwise.

If these particulars are in order, the Registrar will issue a certificate of registration to the limited partnership. Any changes to this information must be notified to the Registrar on Form LP6 (see Appendix 3) within seven days of the change. If a general partner becomes a limited partner or a limited partner assigns their share, this must be advertised in the *London, Edinburgh* or *Belfast Gazette* as appropriate (see below and see further Chapter 16 for contact details for the Gazette and the Registrar of Companies). Until this is done, these transactions have no effect.

Principal place of business in	Register at Companies House in	Official notices to appear in
England or Wales	Cardiff	*London Gazette*
Scotland	Edinburgh	*Edinburgh Gazette*
Northern Ireland	Belfast	*Belfast Gazette*

The Registrar will advise against the use of any name which is the same as, or too like, a name on the register (which includes limited companies and other legal bodies, as well as limited partnerships). The Business Names Act 1985 also applies if the name of a limited partnership does not consist of the names of all the partners. The name must then comply with the rules set out in 3.3.1, disclosure must be made as set out in 3.3.2 and the sanctions described in 3.3.3 apply.

The details registered are available for public inspection at the relevant Companies House.

3.6   Practical advice

The first question to ask is who the client is. If an adviser advises more that one partner, a conflict of interest may arise during the drafting of the agreement, and the different parties may have to be referred to independent solicitors to negotiate the terms. In any event, if the adviser has advised more than one partner and a partnership dispute arises later on, that adviser will almost certainly be unable to act as a result of a conflict of interest.

Whoever you act for, always ensure that you have their instructions on all matters and raise all issues which you consider important, even if these are not specifically raised by the client. A checklist of questions to ask the client(s) could be based on the list of possible clauses for a partnership agreement (see 3.1). Some key questions to consider are as follows:

- what is the objective of the partnership?
- what will the respective responsibilities of the parties be?
- how is the partnership to be financed – by each of the parties and/or outsiders, such as banks?
- how are decisions to be made and what will happen in the event of deadlock?
- how are profits to be distributed?
- are there to be obligations or restrictions on the partners during the time they are partners and/or afterwards?
- will the partners be employing others or subcontracting, and who will have the authority to enter into such contracts?
- how long is the partnership to last and how and on what grounds can it be dissolved?
- what procedure is to be followed by a partner who wishes to leave the partnership?
- what procedure is to be followed in order to expel a partner, and on what grounds may a partner be expelled?

Having once drafted a partnership agreement, clients should be advised that it should be reviewed on a regular basis in order to ensure that it accurately reflects the wishes of the partners. Although, as noted in 3.2, s 19 of the 1890 Act provides that an agreement can be altered by a course of dealing, it is advisable to reflect any changes in the agreement in the interests of certainty. It also ensures that new partners are aware of the agreement applying when they join the firm. If the written agreement is out of date and a new partner is not informed of amendments prior to joining, he cannot consent to them and is not bound by them.

4 Relationship between Partners

4.1 Duty of good faith

Since a partnership is based on mutual trust, it has been established by case law that the partners owe each other a duty of good faith (in the same way, for example, as an employer and an employee owe each other a similar duty). In *Const v Harris* (1924) Turn & R 496, p 525; 37 ER 1191, p 1202, Lord Eldon stated that 'In all partnerships, whether it is expressed in the deed or not, the partners are bound to be true and faithful to each other'.

This means that a partner must act in the interests of the partnership and not for himself. He must therefore act honestly and treat his co partners with the utmost fairness and good faith. This duty should be made clear to all those considering setting up a partnership and borne in mind by them throughout its duration.

The duty of good faith gives rise to a fiduciary relation between partners (*Thompson's Trustee v Heaton* [1974] 1 WLR 605) and therefore they owe each other duties as if they were trustees and the other partners beneficiaries.

The concept of unfair prejudice under s 459 of the Companies Act 1985 has developed from partnership law (see *Re a Company (No 00709 of 1992), O'Neill and Another v Phillips and Others* [1997] 2 All ER 961, per Lord Hoffmann, p 966). An understanding of the duty of good faith in the context of partnerships is therefore vital to an understanding of this important aspect of company law.

4.2   Duties under the 1890 Act

Although the 1890 Act does not expressly set out the duty of good faith, it does set out three requirements which are specific applications of that duty. While the duty of good faith cannot be excluded by agreement, it is possible to exclude by agreement particular aspects of it, including the duties referred to in the 1890 Act.

4.2.1   Duty to disclose information

Section 28 of the 1890 Act provides that a partner must fully disclose 'true accounts and full information of all things affecting the partnership'. This is a positive duty to disclose information, rather than simply a negative duty not to conceal it. In *Law v Law* [1905] 1 Ch 140, one partner bought out the other partner and the partner who had been bought out subsequently discovered that certain assets had not been disclosed. However, at this point the partner who had been bought out accepted the original settlement. The court held that although partners were under a duty to disclose information, the partner who had been bought out was not entitled to compensation for the difference in value of his share of the partnership, because he had validly elected to reach a settlement without full disclosure.

4.2.2   Duty to account for benefits received

Section 29 of the 1890 Act provides that a partner must account to the firm for 'any benefit derived by him without the consent of the other partners from any transaction concerning the partnership, or from any use by him of the partnership property name or business connexion'. For example, in *Bentley v Craven* (1853) 18 Beav 75; 52 ER 29, one of the partners in a sugar refining business, who was entrusted with the buying of sugar, bought a quantity when the price was low and later sold it to the partnership for the then (much higher) market price. The court held that he had to account to the partnership for this profit.

4.2.3   Duty in respect of competing business

Section 30 of the 1890 Act provides that 'If a partner, without the consent of the other partners, carries on any business of the same nature as and competing with that of the firm, he must account for and pay over to the firm all profits made by him in that business'. Technically, therefore, it is permissible to carry on a competing business, provided that the partner does not profit from it, but a partnership agreement should always be drafted to make clear whether and on what terms a partner is permitted to carry on another business.

4.3   Management

Section 24 of the 1890 Act gives various presumptions about the way in which the partnership will be run. These will only apply in so far as a partnership has no contrary agreement:

- s 24(5) provides that every partner may take part in the business. As mentioned in 1.1.3, this is fundamental to the concept of partnership and a partner is unlikely to accept an agreement which excludes this (unless they are a dormant or salaried partner);

- s 24(8) provides that decisions are generally to be taken by a majority of the partners, but that unanimity is required to change the nature of the business;

- s 24(7) provides that unanimity is required to introduce a new partner.

It may be advisable to alter the provisions on decision making so as to counter the possibility of an equality of votes, and to provide for some degree of delegation. If a majority is required, the agreement should specify whether this means a majority by number or on some other basis, for example, by capital contribution. It is also possible to provide for weighted voting (so that greater weight is accorded to the longest serving partners, or those whose capital contribution is greatest).

Details of how often partner meetings will be held, how they will be called, and the quorum, should be specified in the partnership agreement. Provision for a casting vote and for proxy voting should also be considered.

The amount of time to be devoted to the business is not dealt with by the 1890 Act and therefore needs to be specified in a partnership agreement.

4.4   Finance

A partnership will be able to raise money from its partners (as capital, profits retained in the partners' capital accounts or loans) and by way of borrowing from outsiders on the strength of a fixed charge or otherwise (see 2.6).

Section 24 of the 1890 Act also gives various presumptions about the way in which the partnership's finances will be conducted:

- s 24(1) provides that partners share equally in the profits and losses of the business. If a different arrangement is required (for example, to recompense a partner who has contributed a substantial share of the capital or who has more experience or qualifications), this must be specified, preferably in a partnership agreement. In *Joyce v Morissey and Others* (1998) *The Times*, 16 November, which concerned a dispute between the former partners of the pop group The Smiths, the Court of Appeal ruled that the presumption of equality was not displaced by the fact that two of the four partners controlled the management and had a greater commitment to the business. The mere receipt by the other partners of accounts showing a different division of profits was insufficient to show contrary agreement. (Leave to appeal to the House of Lords in this case has been refused.) It is, of course, possible to agree a more sophisticated arrangement than a simple profit share. For example, a stepped arrangement whereby partners move up the scale each year and earn a bigger share of the profits (as happens in many solicitors' firms) may be agreed;

- s 24(1) also provides that partners share equally in the capital (or capital losses) of the business. If capital has not been contributed equally, it is advisable to record how much is contributed by each partner in order to disapply the presumption in s 24(1). In *Popat v Shonchhatra* [1997] 3 All ER 800, two partners in a firm of newsagents made unequal capital contributions, but shared profits and losses equally. The defendant partner, who had made a greater contribution, continued the business alone on the dissolution of the partnership and sold the assets two years later at a profit. The court held that 'profits', in s 24(1), included capital profits (assets over and above the firm's capital), as well as income profits and therefore the proceeds of the assets should be divided equally between the partners;

- s 24(2) provides that the partnership must indemnify the partners for payments made in the ordinary and proper conduct of the partnership business and for anything necessarily done for the preservation of the partnership business or property (see 5.4.2);

- s 24(3) provides that partners may be paid interest on any loan by them to the partnership at 5%. It may be advisable to specify in the loan agreement the rate of interest applicable to the loan, for example, by reference to the prevailing interest rates;

- s 24(4) provides that partners will not receive interest on capital. It is open to the partners to specify to the contrary in the partnership agreement and, as mentioned above, the partners may choose to reflect higher capital contributions by way of an increased share of profits;

- s 24(6) provides that partners are not entitled to a salary. Their income will be in the form of a share of profits, but since they will make drawings during the year against this share, and partnership accounts will not be finalised until after the end of the accounting year, the drawings made by a particular partner are unlikely to represent their exact share of the profits for that year. It may therefore be advisable to specify a limit on the amount of drawings to be taken per month and it is certainly advisable to provide that any drawings taken in excess of the partner's share must be accounted for within a specified period after the end of the accounting year;

- s 24(9) provides that partnership books must be kept at the principal place of business and that every partner has the right to inspect them. This includes the right to use an agent, such as an accountant, to look at the accounts.

Section 42 of the 1890 Act provides an exception to the rule of equality in s 24(1) in the case of certain post-dissolution profits. It states that an outgoing partner (or his estate) is entitled, subject to contrary agreement, at his option to either the share of profits made since his departure, attributable to his share of the assets, or to interest at 5% on that share. In *Barclays Bank Trust Co Ltd v Bluff* [1981] 3 All ER 232, the court ruled that the reference to profits in s 42(1) applied only to income profits accruing in the ordinary course of business, and not to capital profits such as an increase in the value of the partnerships assets. Capital profits after dissolution were therefore to be distributed according to the ratio in which pre-dissolution profits were shared. An outgoing partner was therefore entitled to the increase in value attributable to his share of the capital, as well as to either the profits attributable to that share or 5% interest on it.

4.5 Practical advice

It is important that all partner clients understand the nature of their duties as partners, both those implied by law and those agreed by the partners. If additional duties are to be imposed, it is important that they are workable, and that the agreement sets out the sanctions for failure to fulfil them. The advice to be given in respect of issues of management, decision making and finance must be carefully tailored to the circumstances of a particular partnership in the light of the relative bargaining power of the parties.

5 Liability to Third Parties

Partners will always need to be aware of the existence and scope of their liability, whether under contract, tort, criminal law or otherwise.

5.1 Liability on contracts

According to s 5 of the 1890 Act, every partner is an agent of the partnership and the other partners and, therefore, if a partner acts within his authority, those acts legally bind the partnership and the partners. If a partner, for example, enters into a contract which is within his authority, the partnership will be legally bound to that contract and will have to pay for goods or services supplied under it, or supply goods or services itself if that is what the contract says. Whether a partner has been authorised by the other partners to enter into an obligation on behalf of the partnership is a question of fact, but, even if the partner has not been so authorised, his acts may still bind the partnership under s 5 of the 1890 Act.

Section 5 of the 1890 Act provides that acts of a partner will bind the partnership and the partners if the following conditions are satisfied:

- the partner was 'carrying on in the usual way business of the kind carried on by the firm of which he is a member'. In *Mercantile Credit v Garrod* [1962] 3 All ER 1103, a partnership agreement for a business which let garages and repaired cars expressly excluded the buying and selling of cars. One partner sold a car which he had no right to sell and the buyer sued the firm. The court held that the partnership was liable. In concluding that the partner had done an act which was of the kind done in a garage business, the court looked at 'what was apparent to the outside world in general'. In *Niemann v Niemann* (1890) 43 Ch D 198, a partner accepted, in payment of a debt by a third party to the partnership, shares in a company. The court held that this acceptance did not bind the partnership because it was not a usual method of repayment of a debt;

* the third party knew or believed that the partner had authority;
* the third party knew or believed that the partner was a partner. This is likely to be the case because his name will either be part of the name of the partnership or will appear on the letter heading in compliance with the Business Names Act 1985 (see 3.3).

5.1.1 Specific instances

Beyond these general requirements laid down by s 5, case law has established more specific activities in respect of which partners will automatically be considered to be carrying on business in the usual way.

First, it is within the usual way of all businesses to:

* buy and sell goods in respect of that business (*Bond v Gibson & Jephson* (1808) 1 Camp 185; 170 ER 923);
* receive money in payment of debts and give receipts (*Powell v Brodhurst* [1901] 2 Ch 160);
* employ people (but not to dismiss them, since the employees are employees of all the partners) (*Drake v Beckham* (1843) 11 M & W 315; 152 ER 823);
* obtain information. In *Hamlyn v Houston & Co* [1903] 1 KB 81, a partner in a firm of grain merchants obtained information about another business by bribing one of the other business's employees. The court held the partnership liable in damages, since it was within the partners' authority to obtain information and the means were irrelevant to the question of authority.

Secondly, it is in the usual way of business for partners in trading partnerships (see 1.4.1.1) to:

* bind the firm by negotiable instrument, such as a cheque (*Williamson v Johnson* (1823) 1 B & C 146; 107 ER 55);
* borrow money on the firm's credit (*Higgins v Beauchamp* [1914] 3 KB 1192).

There are certain things which a partner can never have apparent authority to do and, therefore, will only have authority where actually authorised:

* make the firm liable on a deed (an agent who is to make contracts by deed must be appointed as such by deed) (*Steiglitz v Egginton* (1815) Holt NP 141; 71 ER 193);

- give a guarantee on which the firm will be liable (*Brettel v Williams* [1843–60] All ER 702);

- accept payment of a debt by a lesser amount or something which is not money (*Niemann v Niemann*: see above);

- agree to go to arbitration (*Stead v Salt* (1825) 3 Bing 101; 130 ER 452);

- convey partnership land (because s 34 of the Law of Property Act 1925 provides that land is held by up to four partners on trust for all the partners: see 3.4.3);

- consent to judgment against the firm (*Hambridge v De la Crouee* (1846) 3 CB 742; 136 ER 297).

5.2   Liability of partners for other wrongs

A partnership is liable not just for contracts a partner has made, but for certain other acts committed in the course of business.

5.2.1 Torts and crimes

Section 10 of the 1890 Act provides that the partnership is liable for the wrongs which partners commit in the ordinary course of business.

5.2.2 Misapplication of money or property

Section 11 of the 1890 Act provides that, if a partner receives money or property in the course of business and the receipt is within his authority, the partnership is liable to the owner of the money or the property if it is misapplied (see *Bass Brewers Ltd v Appleby and another* [1997] 2 BCLC 700). By way of exception, s 13 of the 1890 Act provides that if the property is trust property and a partner who is a trustee misapplies it by using it in the partnership business, the partnership is not liable unless the other partners are aware of the breach of trust.

5.3   Nature of the liability

As discussed in 1.3.2 and 2.4, partners are personally liable and jointly and severally liable for debts of the firm. Partners must, therefore, contribute their private resources if the partnership assets are insufficient and they can, thus, be sued together or individually if the firm does not pay its debts (see 12.2).

5.4   Duration of the liability

Section 9 of the 1890 Act provides that 'every partner in a firm is liable for all debts and obligations of the firm incurred by the firm while he is a partner'.

5.4.1   Liability on joining the partnership

Liability therefore starts when a partner is admitted to the partnership, and s 17 of the 1890 Act expressly provides that a partner does not become liable, simply by becoming a partner, for debts incurred by the firm before he was a partner. However, he may become liable for such debts if he takes part in a novation or an indemnity (see 5.4.2).

5.4.2   Liability on and after retirement

The question of when liability ends is less straightforward. Section 17 provides that a partner does not cease to become liable for debts incurred by the firm while he was a partner simply by retiring. (In the 1890 Act, the word 'retirement' is used to refer to any partner leaving voluntarily, regardless of the age of the partner.) If there is no agreement as to the duration of the partnership, s 26(1) of the 1890 Act provides that the partnership is 'at will' (see 1.7.1) and, in this case, any partner may retire by giving notice to all other partners. This will result automatically in the dissolution of the partnership. Alternatively, there may be provision for retirement in the partnership agreement, in which case this will govern the procedure for, and the consequences of, retirement.

Subject to contrary agreement, a partner will be liable for all debts and liabilities incurred while he was a partner and, therefore, it is the date a contract was made or a tort committed which is decisive. If it took place before the partner retired, he will still be liable, even where the resulting claim is made after his retirement. In *Bagel v Miller* [1903] 2 KB 212, the estate of a deceased partner was held not liable for goods delivered to the partnership after his death, since the obligation to pay did not arise until delivery.

The only stated exception to s 17 is if there is contrary agreement by way of novation under s 17(3). This sub-section provides that a retiring partner may be discharged from liabilities incurred while he was still a partner if there is an agreement to this effect between the retiring partner, the continuing partners (including any new partners) and the relevant creditor. Such a novation agreement releases the partner from his liability and the creditor can only look to the remaining partners to meet any liabilities. The agreement need not be express. In *Rolfe and Others v Flower, Salting & Co* (1866) LR 1 PC 27, the court held that a creditor of a partnership, by continuing to deal with the partnership in full knowledge of the change of partners, had impliedly agreed to accept the new partnership as debtor in place of the old. Similarly, by not objecting to accounts showing this debt, the new partners had impliedly agreed to accept liability for it. There was, therefore, an implied novation of the debt.

The problems with novation as a method of eliminating liability are that creditors cannot be forced to agree to it and, to release a partner from all liabilities, it is necessary to have a novation in respect of every contract and every claim. Thus, it is of no assistance in respect of tortious claims which are brought only after the partner has retired, but where the cause of action arose while he was a partner.

An alternative method of eliminating liability is to get an indemnity (see, also, 1.6). This is an agreement whereby the remaining partners (and any new ones) undertake to meet the liability of the retiring partner, should any such liability arise in future. It is a form of insurance, since, if the retired partner has to repay a partnership debt, he can recover the amount in full from the other partners. The disadvantage of an indemnity is that the retired partner is still liable to the creditor, and if he cannot trace the partners who gave him an indemnity or they have no money, the indemnity is worthless.

A partner who pays more than his share of a partnership debt is also entitled to recover a contribution from the other partners pursuant to s 24(2) of the 1890 Act (see 4.4). Section 24(2) provides that the partnership must indemnify partners in respect of any payments made by them in the ordinary and proper conduct of partnership business and anything necessarily done for the preservation of the partnership business or property. In *Mathews v Ruggles-Brise* [1911] 1 Ch 194, the court held that the estate of a partner which had paid partnership debts was entitled to recover from the estate of the other partner an indemnity by way of a contribution in proportion to that partner's share of the partnership.

A repudiatory breach of the partnership agreement will not affect the liability of the partners under s 17. In *Hurst v Bryk* [1997] 2 All ER 283, all but one of the partners in a firm of solicitors signed an agreement to dissolve the firm without waiting for the expiration of the notice period provided for by the partnership agreement. The other partner claimed that this amounted to a repudiatory breach of the partnership agreement, which he accepted. The court held that his acceptance of the repudiatory breach did not discharge him from his obligation to contribute to the debts of the partnership (although the judges disagreed on the reason for this).

Appropriate clauses for the partnership agreement

The following clauses are relevant to the retirement of a partner and should always be considered for inclusion in a partnership agreement:

- the partnership will not dissolve on the retirement, death or bankruptcy of a partner (see 8.1.1);
- in the event of a partner retiring, a minimum period of notice should be specified. The considerations here are similar to those set out in 1.7.1 in connection with dissolution;
- this notice period is to be taken as 'garden leave'. In certain partnerships, it may be appropriate to provide that the partner may not continue to work or participate in management during his notice period (but may not start any new employment). This is sometimes referred to as 'garden leave'. It gives some protection to the partnership against attempts by the retiring partner to poach clients or employees. However, such clauses, like all restraint clauses, are subject to certain legal constraints (see 5.4.2.2);
- a partner can be obliged to retire on reaching a specified age, but may be requested to remain;
- the continuing partners have the option to purchase the share of the retiring partner. This may be by lump sum or by instalments with interest;
- mechanism for the calculation of goodwill (see 3.4.6);
- the retiring partner is restrained from soliciting clients of the partnership or setting up a competing business in the same area. Such a clause is subject to certain legal constraints (see 5.4.2.2).

Restraint clauses

The continuing partners cannot simply prevent a former partner from competing with the partnership. As with restrictive covenants in contracts of employment and agreements to sell a business, the existence of a proprietary interest which requires protection must be established, such as confidential information or customer connections, and it must be proved that the restraint imposed is reasonable in its scope. However, although there are no definitive legal rules on the permissible area or duration of restraint, clauses in partnership agreements are more likely to be upheld than those in employment contracts, on the ground of more equal bargaining power. Nevertheless, it is still true to say, for example, that the greater the geographical scope of the restraint clause, the shorter would be the acceptable duration and vice versa.

In *Deacons v Bridge* (see 3.4.6), a restrictive covenant in the partnership agreement of a firm of solicitors in Hong Kong was upheld. The court ruled that it was reasonable, in the interests of the parties, to restrain a partner for five years after leaving the partnership from acting as a solicitor in Hong Kong for clients of the partnership or those who had been clients within three years of the partner's departure. The covenant was in the interests of the public because it benefited clients by promoting continuity in the practice and, by protecting the partnership, encouraged the admission of new partners.

In *Trego v Hunt* (see 3.4.6), the partnership agreement provided that the goodwill was to belong to one partner and the court implied from this a post-termination, non-solicitation covenant of indefinite duration on the part of the other partner. In *Darby v Meehan and Another* (1998) *The Times,* November 25, the partnership agreement provided that a retiring partner was entitled to a share of goodwill and could elect to retain the business of certain clients as part payment of that share, but did not provide for any non-solicitation covenants. The court implied a two year non-solicitation clause on the part of the continuing partners, in relation to the clients retained by the departing partner.

A clause which is too wide may be saved, in part, by severing the invalid elements, but only if they can be severed from the rest of the clause without altering the nature of the agreement and while leaving a clause which makes grammatical sense.

If a restraint clause is to be included in the partnership agreement, specialist advice on the subject should be sought and the latest case law checked.

Notification of retirement

It is in a partner's own interests to notify his retirement to outsiders because s 36 of the 1890 Act states that a partner will continue to be liable to creditors of the firm until they have notice of the change in the firm's constitution. What amounts to notice, in this context, varies for different creditors.

Creditors who have previously dealt with the firm and who knew the retired partner was a partner must receive actual notice of the retirement. This may be in the form of an explanatory letter or a letter with a letter heading from which the partner's name has been deleted. A notice in the *London, Edinburgh* or *Belfast Gazette* (according to the country of the principal place of business: see 3.5), published each weekday, or a newspaper, only constitute notice if the creditor actually sees the notice.

The existence of a notice in the *Gazette* is sufficient notice to those who did not have dealings with the firm while the retired partner was a partner, but who knew or believed that he was a partner. This is so regardless of whether they read it.

Those who only become creditors of the firm after the partner has retired and who do not know that the retired partner was a partner are not entitled to notice of his retirement.

Remaining partners

It is for the retiring partner to make sure that proper notices are given, so that he is not liable under s 14 (see 5.5) or s 36 of the 1890 Act. However, remaining partners should ensure that they comply with the provisions of the Business Names Act 1985 in order to avoid the commission of a civil wrong or criminal offence (see 3.3.3). When a partner retires or a new partner joins, the change in membership should be reflected by a change of partnership name (if the name previously consisted of the names of all the partners and it is intended to alter it to reflect the change in the partners) or a change in the names of the partners listed on all official documents (or, if there are more than 20 and the documents simply refer to a list at the place of business, to that list) in accordance with the Business Names Act 1985.

5.5 Holding out

In addition to actual partners and retired partners who have not given sufficient notice, there is a final category of 'partners' who, though not actually partners, may be liable as such to third parties because they are held out to the outside world as partners. The relevant provision is s 14 of the 1890 Act, which provides that:

> Everyone who by words spoken or written or conduct represents himself, or who knowingly suffers himself to be represented, as a partner in a particular firm, is liable to any one who has, on the faith of any such representation, given credit to the firm.

Typical examples of those who could incur liability by holding out are salaried partners (see 1.6) and other senior employees. However, where the genuine partners hold out a non-partner as a partner or knowingly allow the non-partner to hold himself out, they will also be liable under s 14 because they have represented themselves as partners of the non-partner, or allowed themselves to be so represented.

In either case, liability is limited to claims by a third party to whom the representation has been made and who has relied on the representation to give credit to the firm.

5.6   Comparison of s 14 and s 36

There is an overlap between s 14 and s 36, since both sections apply to non partners who appear to be partners to outsiders and make them liable as such. However, there are three key differences.

First, in order to establish liability under s 14, the third party must act in reliance on the belief that the alleged partner is a partner (whereas, for s 36 to apply, the third party only needs to believe that the retired partner is still a partner and need not consider it important). In *Nationwide Building Society v Lewis and Another* [1998] 2 WLR 915, a firm of solicitors gave negligent advice in a report on title. This was sent under cover of a letter on headed paper which held out an employed solicitor as a partner. The court held that liability under s 14 of the 1890 Act only arose where there had been a holding out, reliance on that holding out and the consequent giving of credit. On the facts, there was no evidence that the building society had noticed the inclusion of the employee's name on the note paper, still less that it had relied on the holding out. Section 14, therefore, did not apply.

In *Hudgell, Yeates & Co v Watson* [1978] 2 All ER 363 (see 8.1.1), a partnership of solicitors which had dissolved automatically through illegality when one partner failed to renew his practicing certificate was reconstituted by conduct among the other partners. The partners were unaware of the failure to renew and, thus, of the dissolution and reconstitution. The former partner was consequently held out as a partner because neither he nor his former partners realised that he was not a partner. However, the plaintiff client had not relied on the holding out, since he had instructed another partner and the unqualified partner was not involved. The plaintiff was, therefore, unable to hold the unqualified partner liable under s 14.

A second difference is that s 14 may apply to anyone, whereas s 36 can only apply to those who were formerly partners. A third difference is that liability will not arise under s 14 if the alleged partner can prove that he did not know or did not consent to being held out as a partner, whereas a retired partner will avoid liability under s 36 by giving the correct notice to creditors.

An example of the potential relationship between the two sections is provided by *Tower Cabinet Co Ltd v Ingram* [1949] 2 KB 397. Mr Ingram and Mr Christmas ran a partnership called 'Merrys' which came to an end. They agreed that Christmas should continue to run Merrys, but that he should not use note paper with Ingram's name on it. In fact, Christmas did use such note paper to confirm a new contract. The court held that Ingram was not liable. He had clearly shown that he did not consent by agreeing that Christmas should not use the old note paper. Since there was no consent, s 14 could not apply. Section 36 could not apply either because the new creditor did not know, prior to Ingram's retirement, that he was a partner.

5.7 Practical advice

Always advise a non–partner client (including a former partner who has retired) to do all they can to ensure that they do not hold themselves out as a partner or allow the partners to do so. For example, if they are named on the firm's note paper, they should ensure that the distinction between their status (whether as an employee, consultant, associate or other) and that of the actual partners is spelled out clearly to avoid any confusion.

If a non–partner is held out by the other partners, he will have a defence if he can show that he did not know or did not consent to the holding out. However, if he knows that his name appears as a partner on the letter heading, then he will be unable to show lack of knowledge of the holding out (which is evidentially difficult in any case) and should, therefore, do something positive to show his lack of consent, for example, by complaining to his ex-partners in writing and sending the letter by recorded delivery.

Similarly, you should advise partners to ensure that they avoid holding out non–partners as partners, or allowing non-partners to hold themselves out as partners, since this could lead to the partnership being liable for the actions of the non–partner.

6 Limiting Liability

As discussed in 1.3.2, 1.3.3 and 5.3, partners are jointly and severally liable for all debts and obligations and this liability is unlimited. However, there are a number of ways in which partners can avoid or, at least, mitigate the effects of unlimited liability and these should be considered when advising any client.

6.1 Limited Partnerships Act 1907

The Limited Partnerships Act 1907 provides that partners may form limited partnerships (which must be registered) in which one or more partners have limited liability, so long as at least one partner has unlimited liability (see 1.4.2 and 3.5).

6.2 Contractual agreement and disclaimers

A partnership may limit its liability and, thus, indirectly, that of the partners, to outsiders by contractual agreement, for example, by use of a capping clause for economic loss due to negligence or by use of a non-contractual disclaimer. In order for a capping or exclusion clause in a contract to be valid, it must be incorporated into the contract and any ambiguity in the clause will be construed against the partnership. Non-contractual disclaimers are only valid if the third party has notice of them.

Such clauses and disclaimers are subject to restrictions under the Unfair Contract Terms Act 1977 (UCTA) and the Unfair Terms in Consumer Contracts Regulations 1994. In addition, they may be commercially unacceptable to certain clients and a partnership which seeks to use them should consider whether their advantages outweigh their disadvantages.

Section 3 of UCTA prevents a contracting party from excluding or restricting its liability for breach of contract where one party deals on the other's written standard terms, unless the exclusion or limitation is reasonable under s 11. Sections 2 and 11 of UCTA require clauses excluding negligence in contracts and disclaimers of negligence liability to be reasonable in order to validly exclude liability for economic loss. In assessing whether a clause is reasonable under s 11 of UCTA, the court is to have regard to a number of factors, including the resources which the defendant could expect to have to meet potential liabilities and the extent to which insurance is available.

The Unfair Terms in Consumer Contracts Regulations only apply to contracts with consumers and, then, only to terms which have not been individually negotiated.

There are additional restrictions on the limiting of liability by certain professional partnerships. For example, s 310 of the Companies Act 1985 makes clauses exempting auditors from liability for breach of duty void and s 60(5) of the Solicitors' Act 1974 makes clauses in contentious business agreements (relating to proceedings in a court or tribunal) exempting solicitors from liability for negligence or any other responsibility void.

6.3   Incorporation

Another method of avoiding unlimited liability is to change the legal structure of the business to a limited liability company. This option is open to all trading partnerships and, increasingly, to professional partnerships. Certain formalities are required in order to incorporate a company (see 2.2) and to transfer the partnership business to the company and issue shares in it to the partners. The exact valuation of a partner's share (see 3.4.5 and 8.3) for the purpose of granting shares in the company will have to be established, since the voting rights of shareholders depend on the percentage of shares held. It will also be necessary to transfer existing insurance policies into the name of the company and novations will be required in order to transfer over contracts.

Corporate status has a number of other advantages and disadvantages (see Chapter 2).

6.4 Limited liability partnerships

In addition to the methods of limiting liability, considered above, it is likely that, in the next few years, the law will be amended to provide for the creation of limited liability partnerships in which partners have limited liability, but also management rights. The topic of limited liability partnerships will be considered at 14.1.

6.5 Practical advice

A more practical way to mitigate the risks of unlimited liability is to manage the risk itself. Tactics which may be adopted include:

- building up goodwill with clients and customers;
- putting in place systems of quality control, including appropriate supervision of employees;
- maintaining adequate insurance;
- assessing the risks before entering into an agreement;
- drafting appropriate contractual terms as to the obligations of the parties (see, also, 6.2).

7 Disputes

Although many disputes among partners are settled informally, this is not always possible. A dispute may be taken to court, but a further alternative is to provide for some form of alternative dispute resolution (ADR), such as arbitration, mediation or conciliation. Such procedures can be used to reach agreement on matters which arise during the currency of an agreement or as a means of allowing for a less destructive parting of the ways.

A dispute may only be submitted to arbitration (or any form of ADR) if all parties agree. Rather than trying to reach agreement when a dispute arises, it is sensible to provide for some form of ADR in the partnership agreement, since, if a dispute cannot be settled internally, it is unlikely that the parties will be able to agree on any ADR procedure at that time.

7.1 Arbitration

An arbitration clause is binding on the parties. If such a clause exists, then the Arbitration Act 1996 provides that the court must grant a stay of any court proceedings if an application for such a stay and a referral to arbitration is made (except in the limited circumstances set out in s 8(4) of that Act). The potential advantages of arbitration are that it can be quicker than going to court and avoids adverse publicity. It can, however, be more expensive as an arbitrator's fees may be considerably greater than those of the court (which is, effectively, subsidised by the State).

The partnership agreement should specify how an arbitrator is to be appointed, what powers he will have and any right of appeal and can, for example, adopt model arbitration rules, such as those used in the construction industry.

The Chartered Institute of Arbitrators maintains a register of qualified arbitrators and can assist in setting up an arbitration (see Chapter 16 for contact details).

7.2   Mediation

The new court procedures which apply to most actions commenced on or after 26 April 1999 mean that the parties will be asked at least twice, during an action, whether or not they have considered methods of ADR and, in particular, mediation. They will be asked once at the beginning of the case and once just before the case goes to a final trial. Thus, even without a clause allowing for mediation, it will become relevant if proceedings are issued.

A meditation clause cannot be used to force a resolution, since participation in mediation is voluntary. However, the attractions of mediation mean that the parties may be willing to try it and a clause in the agreement could reinforce this.

Mediation is a process by which disputing parties engage the assistance of a neutral third party to act as a facilitating intermediary (a mediator). The mediator has no authority to make any binding decisions, but uses various procedures and skills to help the parties to resolve their dispute by negotiated agreement. Two of the main bodies that deal with mediation in the commercial arena are the Centre for Dispute Resolution (CEDR) and the ADR Group (see Chapter 16 for contact details). Both are networks of independent mediators who can provide a range of ADR services.

If there is a genuine will to solve the problem, then mediation can sometimes work where direct negotiation has failed. Even if it seems that the time for talking has passed, the prospect of a long and expensive court case and the permanent loss of a business relationship may increase the chances of mediation succeeding.

The parties have nothing to lose (other than the time and cost involved in the hearing, which is usually scheduled to last for a day or part of one day) and any party may abandon the procedure at any time. As a result, mediation can defuse confrontational situations and lead to a settlement. Even if it does not, the 'brainstorming' exercise undertaken by both parties may remove some of the obstacles to a settlement, give the parties a chance to vent their frustrations by putting their arguments directly to each other and can be useful in the preparation of a case.

7.3   Assignment of a partnership share

Section 24(7) of the 1890 Act provides that all partners must consent to the admission of a partner. Where such consent is not obtained, a partner may still assign his share in the partnership, but s 31(1) of the 1890 Act provides that an assignee is entitled only to a share of the profits and not to manage the firm. In *Re Garwoods Trusts* [1903] 1 Ch 236, the court stressed that an assignee had no right to challenge *bona fide* acts of management and it may, therefore, be that the position would be different if the management were not being carried on in good faith.

Section 31(2) of the 1890 Act provides that, on dissolution (see Chapter 8), an assignee has the right to an account (see 13.4) and to the share of the partnership assets to which the assigning partner would have been entitled.

7.4   Expulsion

This is only possible where the partnership agreement so provides, since s 25 of the 1890 Act states that there is no power to expel unless there is express agreement. Case law has laid down certain conditions which must be satisfied if an expulsion clause is to be valid.

7.4.1   The clause must cover the complaint

In *Snow v Milford* (1868) 18 LT 142; (1868) 16 WR 554, a partnership agreement contained an expulsion clause which referred only to financial improprieties. The complaint which led to the purported expulsion was that the partner 'being a married man, has committed adultery with various persons in the city of Exeter'. The court held that the expulsion was unlawful, since the actual ground relied on was not covered by the expulsion clause in the partnership agreement.

7.4.2   Good faith

The partners must exercise the power to expel in all good faith. In *Blisset v Daniel* (1853) 10 Hare 493; 68 ER 1022, the court held that the expulsion of a partner without cause or explanation was ineffective because it was done in bad faith. The expulsion was not for the benefit of the partnership as a whole, but simply a response to a threat by another partner that he would leave if the expulsion were not carried out.

The question of what procedural requirements must be complied with in order to fulfil this duty has been discussed in several judgments. In *Barnes v Youngs* [1898] 1 Ch 414, a partner was expelled without warning and without being given the chance to explain. It was held that the expulsion could not be effective when carried out in such a way. However, in *Green v Howell* [1910] 1 Ch 495, the court upheld the expulsion of a partner who had not been give a chance to explain. It ruled that *Barnes v Youngs* was not an authority for the proposition that the partner must always be given due warning prior to expulsion, but only that, on the facts of that case, the expelling partners lacked good faith. In *Barnes*, the cause of the expulsion (the partner was living with a woman to whom he was not married) had existed at the outset of the partnership and the other partners had always been aware of this. By contrast, in *Green v Howell*, the breach was so flagrant (diverting profits from the partnership) that the expelled partner must have been aware of what he had done wrong and, therefore, had had ample opportunity of contesting the expulsion. There was, thus, no lack of good faith in the expulsion.

It therefore appears that it is possible to expel a partner summarily where the facts are such that the expelled partner can be in no doubt that he has done something which would render him liable to expulsion. However, the procedure for expulsion should be specified in the partnership agreement and, where possible, the partner should be given due warning and a proper hearing prior to any expulsion.

7.5 Practical advice

If clients seek advice at the outset of their relationship, they should be advised to include in a partnership agreement appropriate clauses to deal with disputes. Such clauses should include some provision for ADR, the grounds and procedure for expulsion and an option for continuing partners to purchase the share of an outgoing partner.

If advice is only sought after the dispute has arisen, any agreement should be carefully checked and followed in respect of provisions governing disputes. Where there are no such provisions, it may be possible to assist them in reaching an agreement. If not, it is still worth suggesting that the dispute be submitted to arbitration or mediation, but, ultimately, court action may be necessary (see Chapter 13). In any event, an adviser should be aware of the possibility of a conflict of interest if he advises more than one partner or has advised other partners in the past (see 3.6).

8 Dissolution

Dissolution marks the end of the partnership as a going concern. If the business is genuinely to come to an end or to be sold, the assets will be collected, the debts paid and any surplus distributed to partners. Alternatively, it may be that one or more of the partners are to continue the business. In this case, the continuing partners will buy out those who are leaving, and effectively continue the same business as a sole trader or partnership.

Section 37 of the 1890 Act provides that a partner can compel the others to publicise the dissolution. This is particularly important where one or more partners are to carry on the business, since the partners who leave are at risk of incurring liability under s 36 of the 1890 Act (see 5.4.2).

8.1 Procedure

A partnership may be dissolved in a number of ways by a partner or by the court.

8.1.1 Non-judicial grounds

Sections 32–34 of the 1890 Act provide that a partnership is dissolved automatically without the involvement of the court in the following situations:

- at the end of fixed period;
- on the achievement of a fixed purpose;
- when notice is given to all partners in a partnership at will (see 1.7.1). This may be varied by contrary agreement and is not applicable to limited partners (see 1.4.2) by virtue of s 6(5)(e) of the Limited Partnerships Act 1907;

- on the death of partner. This may be varied by contrary agreement (and does not apply to the death of a limited partner);

- on the bankruptcy of partner. This may be varied by contrary agreement (and does not apply to the bankruptcy of a limited partner);

- in the event of illegality. This may not be varied by agreement. It may be that the business is unlawful or that it was formed illegally. In *Hudgell, Yeates & Co v Watson* (see 5.6), one partner in a firm of solicitors failed to renew his practice certificate and therefore could not legally practice. It was held that the partnership dissolved at the date the certificate lapsed. Since the other partners continued to practice, a new partnership was constituted by conduct (and excluded the former partner who could not legally practice). However, the partnership will not dissolve just because the objects of the firm could be carried on illegally. In *Dungate v Lee* [1967] 1 All ER 241, a partner in a firm of bookmakers had not obtained the permit necessary to carry on bookmaking. However, the court held that the purpose of the partnership was not illegal and that, as a permit was only required by those partners actually engaged in bookmaking, the partners were not necessarily breaking the law. The partnership had, therefore, not been automatically dissolved;

- when a partner's share is charged to pay a private debt. Section 33 provides that, if this happens, the other partners may dissolve the partnership.

8.1.2 Judicial grounds

Given the extensive grounds for dissolution without court involvement, judicial dissolution is only rarely necessary. For example, where no notice period has been agreed, a partnership at will may simply be dissolved by any of the partners on giving notice to the other partners. Partnerships for a fixed term or purpose may be dissolved on the expiry of the term or achievement of the purpose.

However, judicial dissolution may be required if one or more partners (but not all, since the partners acting unanimously could simply alter the agreement) wish to dissolve a partnership for a fixed purpose or term, or a partnership at will with an agreed notice period, before the purpose is achieved or the term or notice period has expired.

Section 35 of the 1890 Act provides that the grounds on which the court may dissolve the partnership are as follows.

- in the event of the permanent physical incapacity of a partner. A petition may be presented by any other partner;

- where a partner is guilty of conduct prejudicial to the business. This may be conduct relating to the business or outside conduct, such as a criminal conviction for dishonesty relating to a partner's private affairs, but only conduct which affects the business. A petition may be presented by any other partner;

- where a partner wilfully or persistently breaches the agreement (whether written or otherwise). The element of wilfulness requires that there be a serious breach inflicting damage on the firm. A petition may be presented by any other partner;

- where the business can only be carried on at a loss. The losses must not be merely temporary;

- where it is just and equitable that the partnership be dissolved. If the other grounds are not satisfied, the court may nevertheless dissolve the partnership if it is right and fair to do so. Any partner may petition on this ground.

In addition, s 96 of the Mental Health Act 1983 provides that the Court of Protection may order the dissolution of a partnership where a partner is, under s 94 of that Act, 'incapable, by reason of mental disorder, of managing and administering his property and affairs'.

8.1.3 Court declaration

If there is a dispute as to whether the requirements of dissolution have been met, the issue can be settled by the grant of a court declaration on the subject either as part of wider procedures to settle the distribution of assets or separately (see further Chapter 13).

8.2 Winding up

After dissolution, the partnership will be wound up. In circumstances where the dissolution of a partnership has become desirable, the partners may wind up the partnership informally themselves. This will be the appropriate procedure where the partnership is solvent. However, where all partners, as well as the partnership, are insolvent, one of the procedures under the Insolvent Partnerships Order 1994 will be more appropriate, as the position of the partners' private creditors can then be taken into account (see Chapter 9).

Section 38 of the 1890 Act provides that partners bind each other as far as is necessary to wind up the firm and to complete transactions unfinished at time of dissolution. This can include the following:

- receipt of debts due to the partnership (*King v Smith* (1829) [1824–1834] All ER 371);
- completion of contracts (*Butchart v Dresser* (1853) 4 De GM & G 542; 43 ER 619);
- granting a charge to secure a partnership debt (*Re Bourne, Bourne v Bourne* [1906] 2 Ch 427);
- draw cheques on the partnership account (*Backhouse v Charlton* (1878) 8 Ch D 44);
- issue a bankruptcy notice for a judgment obtained by the firm (*Re Hill ex p Holt & Co* [1921] 3 All ER 650).

Any partners actively involved in the winding up may deduct an allowance (*Manley v Sartori* [1926] All ER 661).

8.2.1 Appointment of a receiver and manager

As with all partnership matters, the partners act as agents for each other in the winding up (s 38 of the 1890 Act). Where one or more of the members object to this procedure, an application may be made to the court for a receiver and/or manager to be appointed to conduct the winding up. The function of a receiver is to get in the assets of the partnership and pay the partnership debts, but not to determine the rights of the partners *inter se* or to run the business. The function of a manager is to carry on the business of the partnership under the direction of the court. In practice, where a manager and receiver are appointed, they are likely to be the same person.

An application for the appointment of a receiver may be made (see the CPR Sched 1, re-enacting RSC Ord 30, for details). The court may appoint a receiver if it determines that to do so would be just and equitable and it will take into account the nature of the business and the probable effects of the appointment of a receiver (s 37 of the Supreme Court Act 1981). An application will usually be granted where the partnership has already been dissolved (*Pini v Roncoroni* [1892] 1 Ch 633), but in other instances it will be necessary to show facts which could lead to a judicial dissolution, such as exclusion from management (*Floydd v Cheney* [1970] 2 WLR 314) or misconduct of a partner and jeopardy to partnership assets (*Smith v Jeyes* (1841) 4 Beav 503; 49 ER 433). A member of the partnership may be appointed as the receiver if this is appropriate in all the circumstances.

The appointment commences from the making of the order, and a copy of it must be served on the receiver and all parties. The partners may no longer manage the partnership and an injunction may be granted to restrain them from so doing (*Dixon v Dixon* [1904] 1 Ch 161). The receiver has authority to deal only with the assets of the partnership and not with those of the individual partners (*Boehm v Goodall* [1911] 1 Ch 155). Assets subject to a prior charge are not partnership assets for this purpose (*Choudhri v Palta* [1994] 1 BCLC 184).

8.2.2 Final distribution

Section 39 of the 1890 Act provides that every partner is entitled to have the partnership property applied in satisfaction of the firm's debts. Section 44 of the 1890 Act governs the distribution of the assets, subject to contrary agreement. It provides that the assets of the partnership are to be applied as follows:

- first, to creditors;
- secondly, to partners in respect of any loans made by them to the firm;
- thirdly, to partners in respect of capital contributions;
- fourthly, if there is any residue, to the partners in the same proportions as the profits were shared.

Section 44 also provides that if there are insufficient assets to pay creditors and repay the partners' capital, the deficiency is to be made good, first, out of profits; secondly, out of capital; and, thirdly, by partners personally in their profit sharing ratio. If, therefore, the partnership assets are insufficient to pay debts to creditors or to partners, the partners must make good this deficiency in their profit sharing ratios. However, if partners are required to contribute to make good capital losses and one partner cannot afford to contribute, his share need not be made good by the others (*Garner v Murray* [1904] 1 Ch 57).

These rules only apply if the partnership is solvent. The position on insolvency is considered in Chapter 9.

8.3   How to value partnership property and the partnership

There is no universally agreed formula for assessing the appropriate price to pay for a share in a partnership (or by extension for the partnership itself if the whole business is sold). There are a number of methods of valuing the assets (see 3.4.5), including intellectual property rights and goodwill (see 3.4.6), which, added together, can produce a total valuation for the partnership. The valuation of a particular partner's share may then be assessed on this basis. However, this approach can only give an indicative price and other issues, such as potential profits and liabilities, need to be taken into account. Ultimately, as with other transactions, the correct price is determined by what the buyer is prepared to pay and what the seller is prepared to accept.

If a partnership is being sold, a Sale and Purchase Agreement will need to be drafted, containing the terms on which the business is to be sold, exactly what is being sold and how the purchase price is to be apportioned as between each of the assets being sold. The latter is important for tax reasons, in particular, stamp duty (see 11.5), capital gains tax and associated reliefs (see 11.2).

Where the purchase price is particularly low, the purchaser may be at risk if the sale is considered to be a 'transaction at an undervalue' within the meaning of s 238 or s 423 of the Insolvency Act 1986, since the court could then set aside the transaction (see 9.2.4.1). Where the purchaser acquires assets and assumes responsibility for some but not all of the creditors, this may be seen as a preferential treatment of creditors under s 239 of the Insolvency Act 1986 (see 9.2.4.1) and similarly render the transaction liable to be set aside.

8.4   Limited partnerships

Section 6(5) of the Limited Partnerships Act 1907 provides that a limited partner cannot dissolve the partnership by notice and that neither the death nor the bankruptcy of a limited partner cause dissolution. A limited partner may apply to the court for dissolution (*Re Hughes & Co* [1911] 1 Ch 342), but the mental incapacity of a limited partner will not be a ground for the dissolution of the partnership (s 6(2) of the Limited Partnerships Act 1907).

8.5   Practical advice

When a partnership agreement is drawn up (see Chapter 3), consideration should be given to provisions on dissolution, including duration, notice periods (see 1.7.1), valuation and the use of the partnership name.

If a client seeks advice at a later stage on the dissolution of a partnership, the initial stage of advice should be to consult the partnership agreement if there is one. However, if the procedures which it specifies for dissolution are inadequate, or there are no relevant provisions, or no agreement exists, consideration should be given to all the options available to him. These may include, for example, an attempt to resolve the dispute by mediation (see 7.2) before the expenses of litigation are incurred in what will often be acrimonious circumstances.

9 Insolvency

The law relating to insolvent partnerships is largely to be found in the Insolvent Partnerships Order 1994 SI 1994/2421 (the Order) which applies many of the provisions of the Insolvency Act 1986 (IA 1986). A number of procedures are available to insolvent partnerships, including two designed to assist in the survival of the business (voluntary arrangements and administration orders) and a number of others designed to assist in the termination of the business. The Order refers to 'members', rather than partners, and defines these as partners and those liable under s 14 of the 1890 Act (see 5.5).

It should also be noted that the DTI is currently reviewing insolvency law with particular reference to rescue procedures and bankruptcy.

9.1 Voluntary arrangements

A partnership voluntary arrangement is a scheme for the running of the partnership so as to enable its debts to be paid. Such arrangements are governed by Art 4 and Sched 1 of the Order.

9.1.1 Proposal

A proposal for a voluntary arrangement, accompanied by a statement of affairs, must be made by the partners, unless an administration order, winding up order or joint bankruptcy order has already been made, in which case a voluntary arrangement may only be proposed by the administrator, liquidator or trustee in bankruptcy.

The proposal is made to a nominee (who must be a person qualified to act as an insolvency practitioner) to supervise the implementation of the voluntary arrangement. The nominee named in the proposal will report to the court on whether meetings of creditors and partners should be called and, thus, in effect, will report on whether the proposals are feasible. If the nominee cannot properly prepare his report on the basis of the information in the proposal and the statement of affairs, he may call on the partners to give him further information, including access to the partnership's accounts and records.

The Order does not specify whether the partners have to act unanimously, by a simple majority, or otherwise, in proposing the voluntary arrangement. Section 24 of the 1890 Act states that 'ordinary matters' may be decided by a majority, but that unanimity is required in order to admit a new partner or change the nature of the partnership business (see 4.3). This section draws a distinction between day to day business decisions, which may be taken by a majority, and decisions which affect the fundamental nature of the partnership, where the implied rule is that of unanimity and it seems that the proposal of a voluntary arrangement is more likely to fall into the latter category. However, the best course of action for any partnership would be to include a clause in the partnership agreement which specifies the manner in which such a proposal is to be approved.

9.1.2 Approval

The proposed voluntary arrangement will be implemented if it is approved by three-quarters in value of the creditors and one-half in value of the partners, and the voluntary arrangement then becomes binding on all creditors and partners who had notice of the meeting and were entitled to vote, other than those secured and preferential creditors who did not agree to the voluntary arrangement.

The requirement that a voluntary arrangement be approved by 'one-half in value of the members' (Insolvency Rules 1986 SI 1986/1925, r 1.20) presumably refers to the partners' capital contributions, but it would be advisable to have an express clause in the partnership agreement, since, if the views of certain partners, for instance, the managing or senior partners, have generally been accorded more weight in decision making, this should be reflected on a vote to approve a voluntary arrangement.

Creditors are unlikely to approve a voluntary arrangement if partners remain solvent, but this difficulty may be overcome if the partners' private assets are effectively brought into the voluntary arrangement by the use of concurrent individual voluntary arrangements by individual partners and/or company voluntary arrangements by corporate partners.

The results of the meetings are reported by their chairmen to the court and, if the proposal has been approved, the nominee will become the supervisor of the arrangement, although he may apply to the court for directions (s 7(4)(a) of the Insolvency Act 1986, as modified by Sched 1 of the Order). A proposal which has been approved is still subject to challenge by a dissenting creditor, partner, nominee, administrator, liquidator or trustee in bankruptcy of the partnership, on the ground either of a material irregularity concerning the meetings or of unfair prejudice (not defined in the Order or the IA 1986) to the interests of a creditor, member or contributory. Section 226 of the IA 1986 defines a contributory as a person who is liable to contribute to the assets of the company on winding up. In a partnership, contributories and partners are likely to be the same people.

9.1.3 Advantages and disadvantages

The advantages of a voluntary arrangement are that the procedure is relatively quick and inexpensive and that it may assist in the survival of the business. One disadvantage is that a proposal for a partnership voluntary arrangement may be overtaken by the presentation of a bankruptcy petition or other proceedings against the partnership. It is possible to ward off predatory creditors with an administration order (see 9.2) or the threat of one.

A second disadvantage is that non–assenting preferential and secured creditors, as well as any creditors who did not receive notice of the meeting or who were not entitled to vote, are not bound by the voluntary arrangement; and personal creditors of partners cannot be involved in, and certainly not bound by, a voluntary arrangement, even though, if they obtain judgment on their debt, they can charge that member's share of the partnership assets with that debt (s 23 of the 1890 Act: see 8.1.1). This could result in such creditors being paid off ahead of partnership creditors who are bound by the voluntary arrangement. However, if all partners, as well as the partnership, enter into voluntary arrangements, this disadvantage will disappear.

9.2 Administration orders

These are governed by Art 6 and Sched 2 of the Order.

9.2.1 Petition

One or more creditors of the partnership or the partners themselves (this provision, like that relating to voluntary arrangements (see 9.1.1) raises the question of how many partners are required) may petition the court for an administration order on similar grounds to those applicable to companies. These grounds are that the partnership is unable to pay its debts and that the order would be likely to achieve one or more of:

• the survival of the whole or any part of the undertaking of the partnership as a going concern (see, for example, *Re Kyrris (No 2)* [1998] BPIR 111);

• the approval of a voluntary arrangement; or

• a more advantageous realisation of the partnership property than on a winding up.

A partnership is deemed unable to pay its debts (see ss 222–24 of the IA 1986) if:

• a partnership debt of more than £750 remains unpaid three weeks after a written demand has been served on the partnership; or three weeks after notice of proceedings commenced against a member for a partnership debt has been served on the partnership; or if a judgment debt is unsatisfied; or

• it has been proved to the satisfaction of the court that the partnership is unable to pay its debts or that its assets are less than its liabilities; or

• the partnership has failed to pay a debt of over £750 within three weeks of receiving notification of proceedings against a member for that debt.

The petition must be supported by an affidavit. This must state:

• the petitioner's belief that the partnership is, or is likely to become, unable to pay its debts;

• the grounds for that belief;

• which of the purposes are expected to be achieved;

• the partnership's financial position.

9.2.2 Moratorium

On presentation of the petition, a moratorium is created, which becomes more comprehensive on the making of an order. At both stages, the moratorium prohibits:

• the making of a winding up order;

• the enforcement of security; and

• the taking of proceedings without the permission of the court or the administrator.

Once an order is made, the moratorium also prohibits:

* the appointment of a receiver; and
* the presentation of petitions for bankruptcy or winding up.

9.2.3 The administration

An administrator is appointed to do all things necessary for the management of the partnership and has powers broadly equal to those of a company administrator, although a partnership administrator is unable to dismiss partners, while he is in office, in the same way that company administrators are able to sack directors (but he may exclude them from management). These powers include:

* collecting in partnership property and disposing of it (see *Re Kyrris (No 2)* [1998] BPIR 111, in which the court held that a counterclaim by the partnership was a partnership asset which could be disposed of by the administrator by settling the action);
* borrowing money;
* bringing and defending legal proceedings;
* carrying on the business of the partnership.

The name of the administrator and a statement that he is managing the partnership must appear on all letters, invoices and orders of the partnership and failure to do this renders the administrator and the partners liable to a fine (s 12 of the IA 1986, as amended by Sched 2 of the Order).

A statement of the partnership affairs must be submitted to the administrator within three months of the making of the order (or such longer period as the court may allow) (s 22 of the IA 1986). Section 23 of the IA 1986, which applies by virtue of s 6 of the Order, provides that the administrator must send to the Registrar of Companies and to all creditors a statement of his proposals for achieving the purpose or purposes specified in the order. (In the case of general partnerships, it is unclear whether the requirement to notify the Registrar is a legislative oversight, but this is likely to be the case, since the Registrar has no other dealings with general partnerships.) If the proposals are approved at a meeting of creditors, the administrator must manage the partnership in accordance with them. He may subsequently apply to the court for the order to be discharged.

9.2.4 Advantages and disadvantages

As with voluntary arrangements, one potential advantage of an administration order is that it may assist in ensuring the survival of the business and, in this respect, it has the advantage over a voluntary arrangement of a moratorium. Alternatively, it might improve the position on winding up.

However, an administration order is disadvantageous in that it can prove expensive and lengthy, and certain prior transactions may be set aside (see 9.2.4.1). In addition, the administrator may not deal with partners' personal assets.

Transactions liable to be set aside

Sections 238, 239 and 423 of the IA 1986, as modified by the Order, provide that the administrator of a partnership may apply to the court for certain transactions entered into by the partnership prior to the administration to be set aside. Section 238 of the IA 1986 provides that a transaction at an undervalue (defined as one for which the partnership received no consideration or consideration which was 'significantly less' than that provided by it), entered into within two years of the onset of insolvency (defined as the making of the administration order or the commencement of winding up), may be set aside by the court on the application of the administrator.

Section 239 of the IA 1986 provides that a preference given within six months of the onset of insolvency (or two years, if given to a 'connected person') may be set aside by the court on the application of the administrator. A connected person is defined as including:

- spouse, spouse's relative and spouse of that relative;

- relative and spouse of relative;

- partner, partner's spouse and partner's relative;

- employee.

A preference is defined as anything which the partnership does or allows to be done which has the effect of putting a partnership creditor in a better position, in the event of an insolvency liquidation, than he would otherwise have been.

Section 423 of the IA 1986 provides that any transaction at an undervalue which is made to put assets beyond the reach of a partnership creditor, or to otherwise prejudice such a creditor, may be set aside by the court on the application of the administrator. There is no time limit on the transactions which may be set aside under this section.

These provisions apply equally in respect of a corporate partner which is put into administration (see 9.2.4).

Effect on the partners' personal assets

While the moratorium conferred by an administration order protects the partnership assets, the partners' private assets may still be subject to attack by partnership creditors, since the moratorium does not protect private assets. Just as with voluntary arrangements, the best advice is for all partners to use individual or company voluntary arrangements or company administration orders if at all possible.

9.3 Winding up as an unregistered company

The partnership may be wound up as an unregistered company with concurrent actions against the partners (Arts 8 and 10 and Scheds 4 and 6 of the Order) or without such concurrent actions (Arts 7 and 9 and Sched 3 of the Order). However, if there is any doubt about the partnership's solvency, concurrent actions should be brought, since partners' personal assets will not be available unless the insolvency procedures have been applied to the partners (*Investment and Pensions Advisory Services Ltd v Gray* [1990] BCLC 38).

9.3.1 The petition

Petitioners

The following may petition for an administration order:

- a partner, but only if there are eight or more partners or the court gives leave and the petitioning partner has paid a joint debt of more than £750, in respect of which he has obtained judgment against the partnership and for which he has not been reimbursed by the partnership within three weeks of service on the partnership of a written demand. If there are to be concurrent petitions against all the partners, all partners must be in support;

- a creditor;

- a partnership administrator, supervisor of a voluntary arrangement, liquidator or trustee of an individual partner;

- the Secretary of State, if he considers that, in the light of a report made to him under one of certain listed statutory provisions, it would be expedient in the public interest for a disqualification order to be made, may petition for the partnership to be wound up (see 9.2.3).

Grounds of the petition

The grounds for winding up are as follows:

- the partnership is dissolved, has ceased to carry on business or is only trading to wind up its affairs; or

- it is unable to pay its debts; or

- the court is of the opinion that it is just and equitable that the partnership should be wound up. This is the only ground available to the Secretary of State.

Where a petition is presented against the partnership and all partners concurrently, only the second ground applies and must be proved against all partners.

An inability to pay debts is deemed to be the case, under ss 222 and 224 of the IA 1986 (as modified by Sched 3 of the Order), if:

- a partnership debt of more than £750 remains unpaid three weeks after a written demand on the partnership, or three weeks after notice of proceedings commenced against a member for a partnership debt, has been served on the partnership; or if

- a judgment debt is unsatisfied; or if

- it is proved to the satisfaction of the court that the partnership is unable to pay its debts or that its assets are less than its liabilities.

Where a petition is presented by a partnership administrator, supervisor of a voluntary arrangement, liquidator or trustee of an individual partner, an inability to pay debts may also be proved by the existence of an insolvency order against the partner for whom the petitioner acts (s 221A of the IA 1986, as modified by Sched 3, Pt I, para 3 of the Order).

Jurisdiction

Section 117 of the IA 1986, as modified by Scheds 5 and 6 of the Order, provides that the High Court and the county court have concurrent jurisdiction over the winding up of partnerships, whereas s 117 provides that, in respect of both registered and unregistered companies, the county court has jurisdiction only where the share capital is £120,000 or less.

The district registries of the High Court do not have jurisdiction where concurrent petitions are made (ss 117 and 265 of the IA 1986, as modified by Sched 4, Pt II, para 5 and Sched 6, para 1 of the Order). Since the county court is available, this is not likely to inconvenience petitioners, but any petitioner who does wish to issue proceedings in the High Court may only do so in London.

9.3.2 The winding up

If a winding up order is granted, a liquidator will be appointed to wind up the company.

9.3.3 Application of the Company Directors Disqualification Act 1986

If a partnership is wound up as an unregistered company (with or without concurrent petitions against partners), each officer of the partnership is potentially liable under the Company Directors Disqualification Act 1986 (CDDA).

Section 16 and Sched 8 of the Order provide that the court may make a disqualification order under the CDDA if it is satisfied that the conduct of an officer of an insolvent partnership (defined as a partner or a person with management or control of the partnership), either in relation to that partnership alone or when taken together with conduct as a director or partner in another business, makes him unfit to be concerned in the management of a company. In addition, s 8 of the CDDA, as modified by the Order, provides that the Secretary of State may also apply for a disqualification order if he considers it to be in the public interest for such an order to be made.

Section 10 of the CDDA provides that the court may also make a disqualification order against a partner who has been ordered to contribute to the partnership's assets under s 213 or 214 of the IA 1986 (see 9.3.5). A partner may be disqualified from being a company director for a period of up to 15 years (ss 6 and 8 of the IA 1986, as modified by the Order). Section 15 of the CDDA provides that, if a partner who is subject to a disqualification order acts in contravention of that order, he may also become personally liable for the debts of the company with which he is involved.

It is not clear whether a partner against whom a disqualification order under the CDDA is made is, thereby, disqualified from remaining or becoming a partner, or is even forced to disclose the existence of the order to any new partnership he may join. However, such an order can only have been made where the partnership has become insolvent and, in those circumstances, it is likely that the partner will have been made bankrupt. Section 360 of the IA 1986 and Pt II of the Insolvency

Proceedings (Monetary Limits) Order 1986 SI 1986/1996 provide that a bankrupt may not obtain credit exceeding £250 or trade without disclosing the fact of his bankruptcy. In practice, this is likely to limit substantially the number of partners who, whilst subject to a disqualification order, are able to practice in partnership.

9.3.4 Transactions liable to be set aside

Sections 238, 239 and 423 of the IA 1986 apply on winding up as on administration (see 9.2.4.1).

These provisions apply equally in respect of a corporate partner which is wound up.

9.3.5 Fraudulent and wrongful trading

Section 213 of the IA 1986 provides that, if, in the course of winding up, it appears that the partnership business has been carried on with intent to defraud creditors or for any other fraudulent purpose, the court may, on the application of the liquidator, order those who were knowingly parties to such carrying on of the business to contribute to the partnership assets.

Section 214 of the IA 1986 provides that, if, in the course of winding up, it appears that the partnership is insolvent and that, at some time prior to the winding up, a partner knew or ought to have concluded that there was no reasonable prospect of avoiding insolvent liquidation, the court may, on the application of the liquidator, order that partner to contribute to the partnership assets. It is a defence to an application under s 214 of the IA 1986 that the partner took every step that he ought to have taken to minimise the potential losses to the partnership creditors and, in assessing this, his knowledge skill and experience, and those expected of a person in his position will be taken into consideration.

These provisions apply equally in respect of a corporate partner which is wound up.

9.3.6 Distribution of assets

Under the s 175 of the IA 1986, the expenses of the winding up are to be paid first, followed by the preferential debts. Rule 4.181 of the Insolvency Rules provides that other debts are to rank equally and s 189 of the IA 1986 states that interest on debts is payable after the debts themselves have been paid. Any surplus will be distributed amongst 'the persons entitled to it' (s 154 of the IA 1986 Act), that is to say, the partners.

There is no provision for loans by partners to the partnership to rank behind other debts as there is in the Partnership Act (s 44: see 8.2.2). Where an insolvent partnership is concerned, this could work considerable injustice to the outside creditors.

The Order provides that, where the joint estate of the partnership is insufficient to meet its debts, those debts rank equally with personal debts in the estates of the partners (ss 175 and 328 of the IA 1986, as modified by Sched 4, Pt II, para 23: see 3.4.1). This does not operate in reverse and private creditors may only share in the partnership assets after the partnership creditors have been repaid.

9.4   Joint bankruptcy petitions

Where the partnership is insolvent and all the partners are individuals with none being limited partners all the partners may, instead of winding up the partnership, present a joint bankruptcy petition on the ground that the partnership is unable to pay its debts (Art 11 and Sched 7 of the Order).

The petition may be presented to the High Court in London (but not to a district registry) or to a county court provided that, in the case of a county court, the partnership had a principal place of business in its insolvency district. Although the estate of each partner will be dealt with separately, a single trustee will be appointed to deal with all the estates. This procedure is not available to creditors who must instead present petitions against one or more partners individually and, if a creditor brings bankruptcy petitions against more than one partner, the court may consolidate such actions (see s 303 of the IA 1986, as modified by Art 14 of the Order).

The Official Receiver becomes the trustee in bankruptcy of all the partners, although he may call a creditors' meeting, or be requested to do so, to appoint a different trustee. A joint meeting of the creditors of the partners and those of the partnership may establish a creditors' committee to act as both a creditors' committee for each partner and a liquidation committee for the partnership (ss 301 and 301A of the IA 1986, as modified by Sched 8, para 18 of the Order). The trustee will realise and distribute the estates of the partnership and the partners (s 305, as modified by Sched 8, para 19).

The priorities on a distribution of assets are set out in ss 328 and 328A of the IA 1986 (as modified by Sched 7 of the Order). Sections 328 and 328A state that the priorities are for each estate:

- its bankruptcy expenses;
- its preferential debts;
- its other debts;
- interest on those debts;
- its postponed debts;
- interest on those postponed debts; and, finally,
- any adjustment between the partners.

If the joint estate is insufficient to meet joint debts, those debts rank equally with personal debts in the estates of the partners (see 3.4.1). As with winding up, this does not operate in reverse and only if there is a surplus after the debts of the joint estate are paid will the partners' estates receive anything from the joint estate.

An advantage of this procedure, which should not be underestimated, is that the CDDA does not apply (see 9.3.3) and the only transactions which are liable to be set aside are those to which s 423 of the IA 1986 applies (see 9.2.4.1). Neither s 213 nor s 214 of the IA 1986 (see 9.3.5) apply.

9.5   Petitions against individual partners

The principle of joint and several liability (see 1.3.3 and 5.3) means that a petition for bankruptcy or winding up may be presented against a single partner by a partnerships creditor (see, for example, *Schooler v Customs and Excise Commissioners* [1995] 2 BCLC 610). Indeed, Art 19(5) of the Order provides that a partnership creditor may present a petition against one or more partners without including them all or petitioning for the winding up of the partnership.

9.6   Limited partnerships

The procedures outlined above and the comments made on them apply equally to limited partnerships under the Limited Partnerships Act 1907, with the following exceptions:

- a joint bankruptcy petition may not be presented (s 264 of the IA 1986, as modified by Sched 7 of the Order). The assets of a limited partner are not available to partnership creditors and it would, therefore, be impossible for that partner's estate to be administered jointly with those of the partnership and the other partners;

- it will rarely be appropriate to present a concurrent insolvency petition against a limited partner, since the insolvency of the partnership is unlikely to affect the solvency of such a partner;

- although all partners, including limited partners, are deemed to be officers of the partnership for the purposes of the CDDA, by their very nature, such partners are less likely than other partners to have been engaged in any conduct which would indicate their unfitness to manage a company. However, the matters to be taken into account when determining unfitness specifically include the breach of certain provisions under the Limited Partnerships Act 1907 (CDDA, Sched 1, Pt 1, para 6, as modified by the Order, Sched 8) and so the disqualification of a limited partner therefore remains a possibility.

9.7 Practical advice

Insolvency is an area where specialist advice should be sought and, if an adviser cannot provide that advice, clients should be made aware of that fact. It is also important to draw to their attention the need to seek this advice promptly and the penalties which may be imposed if they fail to do so or fail to heed the advice.

The Law Society has issued a consultation document (*Multi-Disciplinary Practices – Why? Why not?*, 1998) on multi-disciplinary partnerships. The key questions left open are whether non-lawyer partners should be members of approved professions, whether lawyers should control the MDP, whether The Law Society should regulate the whole MDP or just the solicitors within it and the extent to which client protection provisions should apply. If The Law Society does not regulate the whole MDP, it will be impossible to ensure that current rules providing protection for client money, client confidentiality and appropriate rules on conflicts of interest will apply.

At present, the position is that a firm of solicitors can have a close association with a firm of non-lawyers with a referral arrangement, but must maintain its independence and may not share its fees with non-lawyers (the Solicitors' Introduction and Referral Code). A single combined business is only possible between a solicitor and a non-lawyer if the business is not a solicitor's practice or if the solicitor is employed by the non-lawyers and does legal work for customers other than as a practising solicitor (the Solicitors' Separate Business Code) or if it is a non-legal business.

In practice, MDP type arrangements are already emerging. For example, several of the major accountancy firms have 'sponsored' independent legal practices, including practices elsewhere in Europe, which have management independence, but which share resources and agree to refer work.

10.3 Practical advice

When advising professional clients, it is important to remember that they will be governed not only by the general law of partnership (and, in the future, by LLP legislation if they decide to set up an LLP), but also by the rules of their professional body. The relevant body should always be consulted in order to ascertain the current rules and guidelines and, unless the adviser has specialist knowledge of these, they should refer the client to the relevant professional body. Most such bodies have helplines which their members can use to seek advice on issues of professional regulation and insurance requirements.

11 Taxation of Partnerships

It is clearly beyond the scope of a general book, such as this, to discuss taxation of partnerships in detail. The existing tax treatment, relevant tax rates and other such matters must always be checked before advice is given. However, a number of basic points may be made.

11.1 Income tax

The taxation of partnership income has undergone a number of changes in recent years.

11.1.1 The basis of assessment

The Finance Act 1994 provides that Sched D (contained in s 18 of the Income and Corporation Taxes Act 1988) dealing with profits from a trade (Case I), profession or vocation (Case II) is no longer to operate on the preceding year basis (taxing profits made in the accounting period which ended in the previous tax year), but on the current year basis (taxing profits made in the accounting period which ended in the current tax year), in line with the other income tax schedules. The Finance Act 1994 provided that the basis of assessment under Sched D would be changed with effect from the 1997–98 tax year onwards, although it would apply from the outset for businesses commencing on or after 6 April 1994.

11.1.2 Opening and closing year rules

As a result of the changes to the basis of assessment, the special rules which applied to the opening and closing years of the partnership have been altered and it is no longer open to the Inland Revenue or the taxpaying partner to elect for an alternative form of assessment in those years as they were previously able to.

The rules are now as follows:

1st year	The partners are taxed on the profits from the date of commencement to the following 5 April.
2nd year	The partners are taxed on the profits of the first 12 months (that is, from the date of commencement). This is the current year basis.
3rd and subsequent years	Current year basis.
Final year	The partners are taxed on the profits from the end of the previous accounting period to the date of discontinuance of the partnership business.

These rules may mean that, in the opening and closings years of the partnership, the same profits are taxed twice. If this is the case, overlap relief may be available.

11.1.3 Discontinuance

Partnerships were previously deemed to discontinue when a partner left or died and, therefore, had to make an election to be treated as continuing. However, the Finance Act 1994, amending s 113(1) of the Income and Corporation Taxes Act 1988, provides that only actual discontinuance of the business will now be recognised and, therefore, partners no longer need to make an election.

11.1.4 Personal assessment

The Finance Act 1994 provides that, from the tax year 1997–98 onwards, there will no longer be a joint assessment to tax in the partnership's name upon which partners are jointly and severally liable. Instead, partners will be taxed under the self-assessment regime and each partner will include his share of partnership income in his personal tax return and be solely liable for the income tax liability. In addition, however, a partnership may be required to file a return relating to the partnership as a whole for the purpose of indicating the total taxable profit of the partnership and its allocation between partners (s 12AA of the Taxes Management Act 1970). This will usually have to be filed by 31 January after the end of the relevant tax year.

11.1.5 Computation of profits for income tax purposes

Section 42(1) of the Finance Act 1998 provides that, from the start of the first accounting period, which begins after 6 April 1999, profits of a trade, occupation or profession must be computed on the full earnings basis. Firms must show a 'true and fair view' of their finances for tax purposes, which will include work in progress (where the partnership supplies services) and/or trading stock (where goods are supplied). These changes will affect, therefore, all firms which previously calculated profits on a basis which did not recognise work in progress in full.

11.1.6 Income tax relief

Where a partnership makes a loss, there will be a nil tax assessment for the period in which the loss is incurred (s 380 of the Income and Corporation Taxes Act 1988). Interest paid on loans may be tax deductible.

11.2 Capital gains tax

Partners are individually liable for capital gains tax (CGT) where a partnership asset is disposed of at a chargeable gain. Such a disposal by a partnership is treated as a disposal by each of the partners of their share of the asset and the assessment for CGT is, therefore, made for each partner in the proportion that they own the partnership assets. This proportion is determined according to the partnership agreement or, if none, by s 24 of the 1890 Act (see 4.4).

(The CGT situation of partners in relation to disposal of partnership assets is governed by three Inland Revenue Practice Statements: D12, 1/79 and 1/89).

11.2.1 Relief from CGT

Various reliefs may be available. Replacement of business assets relief (sometimes known as replacement rollover relief) (see s 155 of the Taxation of Chargeable Gains Act 1992 Act) is potentially available if a replacement business asset (land, buildings, ships, hovercraft and aircraft) is acquired one year or less before, or three years after, the disposal of the original business asset. Any gain made on the disposal of the original asset is deferred and 'rolled over' into the new asset until that asset is disposed of.

Retirement relief (see s 163–34 and Sched 6 of the 1992 Act) is potentially available if a partner is 50 years of age or over or in ill health and disposing of all his interest in the partnership. It applies to all or part of the gains on the disposal of chargeable business assets (assets used for the purposes of the business) up to a maximum financial limit after 10 years ownership. Above that limit (£200,000 for 1999–2000), and up to a further limit (£1,000,000 for 1999–2000), gains may be reduced by 50%. If the asset has been owned for less than 10 years, relief will be given on a sliding scale.

Holdover relief (see s 58 and 165 of the 1992 Act) is potentially available where a business asset is given away and (subject to certain exceptions: see s 165(1)(b) of the 1992 Act) both parties agree to defer the tax until sale of the asset by the donee.

11.3 Inheritance tax

Inheritance tax (IHT) may be chargeable on transfers which diminish the value of the estate of the transferor made during the lifetime of a transferor and on the estate of a deceased transferor. It may be payable either immediately or, in the case of most lifetime transfers, only if the transferor does not survive for more than seven years after making the transfer. These rules apply equally where the transferor is a partner.

There will be no IHT liability if the Inland Revenue is satisfied that the market price has been paid for the property. IHT business property relief may be available and IHT may be paid in interest free instalments (s 227 of the Inheritance Tax Act 1984).

11.4 Value added tax

Section 45 of the Value Added Tax Act 1994 (VAT Act) provides that a supplier must be registered for VAT if the supply of certain taxable supplies of goods or services by it exceeds a certain figure (£51,000 from 1 April 1999) in a 12 month period. The VAT Act lists those supplies which are taxable and those which are not. The supplier must then charge VAT at the prevailing rate (currently 17.5% for most taxable supplies) to its customers and account for this to Her Magesty's Customs and Excise.

11.5 Stamp duty

Under the Stamp Act 1891, as amended, stamp duty is payable on certain documents. It is not payable on the underlying transactions and, therefore, it is not payable on the transfer of assets by physical delivery, rather than by written instrument, where this is possible. Documents on which stamp duty is payable include contracts and conveyances both on sale and not on sale. Stamp duty may, therefore, be chargeable, for example, on documents effecting the sale of the partnership business or the sale of a partner's share. The rate of duty varies according to the nature of the document and, in some cases, is a fixed amount per document, while, in others, it is charged *ad valorem* (according to the value of the assets to which the document relates).

11.6 Practical advice

Taxation is an area of law which requires specialist advice and, if the adviser cannot provide that advice, it is important that the client is made aware of that fact or the adviser risks incurring liability to the client (see *Hurlingham Estates v Wilde and Partners* [1997] STC 626, see 2.11).

It is also essential that such advice be sought on a regular basis in order to respond to changes in the law or Inland Revenue practice.

12 Actions by and against Partners

12.1 Jurisdiction

The new Civil Procedure Rules (CPR) and associated Practice Directions (PDs), in force from 26 April 1999, have had a profound effect upon the jurisdiction and procedures of the High Court and county court for all claims, including those involving partners and partnerships. For example, a claim for the recovery of money should now only be commenced in the High Court if the claimant (formerly the plaintiff) expects to recover more that £15,000 (CPR Pt 7 and PD 7, para 2.1).

The CPR Pt 1 sets out the overriding objective of the new system established by the CPR. That overriding objective is to enable the courts to deal with matters justly, including, so far as practicable, endeavouring to ensure:

- that the parties are on an equal footing;
- proportionality with regard to:
  - the value of the claim;
  - its importance;
  - its complexity;
  - the financial standing of the parties;
- a fair and expeditious disposal of the case; and
- the allocation of an appropriate share of the court's resources while taking into account the needs of other cases.

This overriding objective will significantly affect the court's management of actions in all areas, including, for example, disclosure of documents and the timetable for the action. The rules in the CPR will apply to all proceedings involving partners whether in the county court or the High Court. The CPR should be consulted to determine the allocation of the case to the appropriate case management track.

Schedule 1 of the CPR re-enacts, *inter alia*, RSC Ord 81, which sets out detailed rules on proceedings by and against partners and partnerships, whilst Sched 2 of the CPR re-enacts the corresponding provisions of CCR Ord 5 r 9, CCR Ord 25 r 9 on enforcement of judgments or orders against a firm and CCR Ord 25 r 10 on enforcing judgments between a firm and its members (see 2.3 and 12.2). In proceedings involving a firm, both schedules allow for service of a notice seeking the names of the partners at the time relevant to the facts in dispute in the action.

At present, the new procedures in the CPR have still to be fully tested in practice. However, certain areas of ambiguity are evident in the CPR as first published and these are highlighted in this chapter and Chapter 13. Reference should always be made to the CPR and the PDs themselves, together with any update, in order to determine the latest position and care should be taken when using the new court forms which currently contain, in places, errors or statements which are not fully comprehensive. For example:

- Form N1A (notes for the claimant on the claim form), in its note for the claimant on service on a firm, advises that a partner's residential address may be used, whereas CPR Pt 6 and the note in N1A for service on an individual partner state more fully that service may be effected at the usual or last known residential address;

- whilst there appear to be different rules as to who may accept service on behalf of a partnership in the High Court and the county court (see 12.3), the Acknowledgment of Service Forms (N9 and N212) make no reference to this and do not identify who should complete the form;

- Form N211 (claim form – Additional Claims CPR Pt 20) advises the defendant on the use of Form 212, which it defines as an Acknowledgement of Service for Part 20 Claims when, in fact, the correct form is Form N213.

12.2 Action in the partnership name or by or against individuals

As mentioned in 2.3 and 12.1, CPR Scheds 1 and 2 re-enact RSC Ord 81 r 1 and CCR Ord 5 r 9, which provide that two or more alleged partners of a partnership within the jurisdiction may sue or be sued in the partnership name. However, a partnership may still be correctly sued in the name of all the partners, in their capacity as partners (*Oxnard Financing SA v Rahn and Others* [1998] 3 All ER 19).

Although one partner may sue in the partnership name without the consent of the other partners, the court may stay the action until the partner has given his co-partners a full indemnity against all costs (*Seal and Edgelaw v Kingston* [1908] 2 KB 579). Similarly, one or more partners may be sued individually, but they can insist on the other partners being made parties if they are within the jurisdiction, unless they cannot be found (*Robinson v Geisel* [1894] 2 QB 685: see 1.3.3).

Section 3 of the Civil Liability (Contributions) Act 1978 provides that a judgment against one defendant is no bar to an action against another defendant who is jointly liable (see 1.3.3). However, this does not preclude the application of the general principle that the discharge of one joint debtor by accordance and satisfaction discharges all others (*Morris v Wentworth-Stanley* [1999] 1 FLR 83).

12.3 Service of the claim form and particulars of claim

Service may be effected on the partnership by:

- personal service. This may be effected by leaving the claim form with any of the partners or the person having the control or management of the partnership business at its principal place of business at the time of service (CPR Pt 6 r 6.4(5)). If the claim form is served on a person at the principal or last known address of the partnership, it must be accompanied by a written notice stating whether the recipient is served as a partner, the person having control or management or both (PD 6, para 4.2);

- first class post to the address given for service;

- leaving the documents at the address given for service.

  Where no such address is given, the claim should be sent by first class post to, or left at, the usual or last known residential address of a partner or the principal or last known place of business of the partnership (CPR Pt 6 r 6.5(6));

- document exchange if the partnership has a DX address and has not indicated that it will not accept service by this means;

- fax;

- e-mail.

Service by fax or e-mail is only permissible if a willingness to accept service by the chosen method has been indicated in writing by the partnership. Merely having these details on the partnership note paper is not enough. A clear statement of willingness to accept service by these methods is required. As a matter of good practice, if e-mail or fax is used, service should also be effected by a non-electronic method.

If the partnership has been dissolved and the claimant is aware of this, he must serve the claim form on all those sought to be made liable.

12.4 Acknowledging service

Under the CPR, defendants may file and serve an acknowledgment of service in the High Court and the county court where they wish to challenge jurisdiction (for example, if they argue that a valid agreement to take the matter to arbitration exists) or to obtain further time for the filing of a defence. The new 'Response Pack' in N9 contains an acknowledgment of service for this purpose.

The rules on acknowledging service are set out in CPR Pt 10, PD 10 and, in so far as the High Court procedure is concerned, Sched 1 of the CPR, which contains RSC Ord 81 (because CPR Pt 10 r 10.5 notes that RSC Ord 81 in Sched 1 makes special provision in relation to the acknowledgment of service in a claim against a firm in the High Court).

RSC Ord 81 provides for an acknowledgment of service to be completed only by partners in the firm and provides that a person served who is not a partner may return the acknowledgment of service indicating that he is not, and was not, at all material times, a partner in the firm. However, PD 10, para 4.4 provides that, where the defendant is a partnership, service may be acknowledged by the signature on the acknowledgment of service of any of the partners *or* a person having management or control of the partnership business (authors' emphasis).

Presumably, the fact that CPR Pt 10 r 10.5 refers to RSC Ord 81 means that the latter takes precedence over PD, para 4.4. However, the position is unclear, particularly since CPR Pt 50 r 50(2) merely provides that 'These rules apply in relation to the proceedings to which the schedules [which include RSC Ord 81] apply, subject to the provisions in the schedules and the relevant Practice Directions' without establishing which takes precedence.

12.5 Execution

Where judgment is given against a partnership sued in the firm name, execution may issue without leave (CPR Scheds 1 and 2, re-enacting RSC Ord 81 r 5 and CCR Ord 25 r 9) against:

- partnership property within the jurisdiction;
- any person who acknowledged service of the claim form as a partner or who was served as such and failed to do so;
- any person who admitted to being a partner in his pleading;
- any person who was adjudged to be a partner.

12.6 Limited partnerships

The CPR make no separate reference to limited partnerships and, therefore, it would appear that the rules applicable to partnerships generally, which are referred to both as partnerships and as firms in the CPR, also apply to limited partnerships. However, given the unique position of limited partners, it would be surprising if there were no difference in the applicable law. It may, therefore, be that the notes to RSC Ord 81 (which have not been reproduced in Sched 1 of the CPR) are still relevant. Those notes, in the 1999 'White Book', made the following 'suggestions' as to the position with regard to limited partnerships in the absence of express rules in the Limited Partnerships Act 1907 or the RSC;

- a limited partnership may not sue or be sued in the name of the partners, followed by the wording 'trading as [name of firm]'. This is because a limited partnership is registered as an entity. It may, however, sue or be sued in the firm name, since RSC Ord 81 provides that partners may be sued in the name of the firm and s 3 of the Limited Partnerships Act 1907 provides that the word 'firm' includes limited partnerships as well as general partnerships;
- the claim form may not be served on a limited partner, since s 6 of the Limited Partnerships Act 1907 (see 1.4.2) may mean that the firm cannot be bound by the service of legal process on a limited partner. The claim form should, therefore, be served only on a general partner or the person with management or control of the business;
- a limited partner need not acknowledge service, but may do so. (Section 6 of the Limited Partnership Act 1907 only prohibits limited partners from taking part in the management of the partnership

business, which is defined under s 3 of that Act, applying s 45 of the 1890 Act, as 'every trade, occupation or profession' and this does not appear to include defending an action.) However, it may be inadvisable because it may enable an order to be obtained for judgment against him (see below);

- judgment may not be enforced on a limited partner. Section 4 of the Limited Partnerships Act provides that limited partners are only liable to the extent of their capital contribution and, therefore, in principle, judgment against the firm may not be enforced on a limited partner. However, if a limited partner has acknowledged service, it may be possible to obtain an order for execution against him.

12.7 Practical advice

It is usually more appropriate to bring actions against all partners, whether in the firm name or not, since this maximises the assets available to the claimant without recourse to further proceedings if judgment is obtained. It also avoids any possible arguments on election (which could lead to a finding that the claimant has given up his rights against the partner or partners that he did not sue in earlier proceedings for the same relief). However, the client may have valid reasons for not wishing to sue one or more partners (for example, a continuing business relationship). Clear instructions from the client on the course of action desired are needed and equally clear advice on the consequences and risks of that course of action should be given.

In relation to actions by a partnership, it is prudent to seek the consent of all partners before proceeding, both to avoid the need for the instructing partners to provide an indemnity to the other partners (see 12.2) and to ensure that the action does not cause dissension among the partners.

In actions involving limited partnerships, care should be taken in view of the uncertain position under the CPR in relation to court proceedings involving such partnerships.

13 Actions between Partners

13.1 Jurisdiction

The comments made in 12.1 concerning the new CPR apply equally to this chapter.

Actions for the dissolution of partnerships or the taking of partnership or other accounts may only be brought in the Chancery Division of the High Court (with the claim form marked 'Chancery Division') or in the county court (with the claim form marked 'Chancery business'), except for dissolution proceedings involving a partner under a mental incapacity which may also be brought in the Court of Protection (see 8.1.2).

The county court only has jurisdiction over equity claims (defined by s 23 of the County Courts Act 1984 as including partnership dissolution and winding up proceedings) where the value of the property to be dealt with is less than £30,000.

The court can also order the appointment of a receiver and/or an injunction to restrain a partner from breaching his obligations, or to restrain the partners from excluding a partner from management or to prevent serious harm to the partnership.

Where the action is not for dissolution or winding up, it may be brought by or against a representative of partners with a common interest (CPR Scheds 1 and 2, re-enacting RSC Ord 15 r 12 and CCR Ord 5 r 5).

13.2 Action for dissolution

In terms of jurisdiction, it may be more sensible to bring proceedings in the county court where this is possible, as not all district registries of the High Court have Chancery jurisdiction, whereas county court proceedings may be commenced locally to the partnership, the partners and their solicitors.

The grounds for dissolution by the court have been discussed in 8.1.2. The court will generally direct a sale of partnership assets on dissolution unless there is agreement to the contrary and a receiver or receiver and manager may be appointed until sale (see 8.2.1). In exceptional circumstances, the court can order that a partner is bought out at an agreed price. For example, in *Syers v Syers* (1876) 1 App Cas 174, the court ruled that a partner who owned an eighth of the main partnership asset was not entitled to a sale of the business, but only to be bought out.

13.3 Action for an injunction

Section 37 of the Supreme Court Act 1981 provides that the court may grant an injunction where it is just and equitable to do so. Such an action may be brought in connection with an action for dissolution or independently. Injunctions may be granted, for example, to:

*   preserve the assets (*Alder v Fouracre* (1818) 3 Swan 489; 36 ER 947);
*   restrain a partner from interfering with the work of the receiver or the winding up (*Dixon v Dixon* [1904] 1 Ch 161);
*   restrain a partner from breaching the partnership agreement (*Morris v Colman* (1812) 18 Ves 437; 2 Ves 535; 34 ER 383 and 1214);
*   restrain a partner from carrying on business in competition (*England v Curling* (1844) 8 Beav 129; 50 ER 51; *Aas v Bentham* [1891] 2 Ch 244);
*   restrain a partner from copying and removing confidential information (*Floydd v Cheney* [1970] Ch 602).

However, since an injunction is an equitable remedy, the partner seeking the injunction must be prepared to perform his own obligations (*Littlewood v Caldwell* (1822) 11 Price 97; 147 ER 413).

Where there is evidence of a real risk that a partner intends to remove the assets from the jurisdiction or deal with them to the prejudice of the winding up, a co-partner may apply without notice for a freezing injunction (formerly known as a Mareva injunction), restraining the removal of or dealing with the property (see CPR Pt 25 r 25.1(1)(f) and PD 25).

13.4 Action for an account

Section 28 of the 1890 Act imposes a duty on partners to render true accounts (see, also, 4.2.1) and s 44 provides for an account to be taken on dissolution. In *Green v Hertzog* [1954] 1 WLR 1309, the Court of Appeal held that a loan made by a partner to a partnership could only be recovered by the taking of an account under s 44 of the 1890 Act and not by a private action against the other partners.

The taking of an account can, therefore, be either an ancillary remedy on dissolution or an independent remedy in its own right. For example, it may be sought where a partner is excluded from the business (*Harrison v Armitage* (1819) 4 Madd 143; 56 ER 661; *Richards v Davies* (1831) 2 Russ & M 347; 39 ER 427).

A partner may seek a general account of the dealings and transactions of the partnership business or a limited account of a particular transaction or set of transactions.

CPR Pt 25 and PD 25 (accounts and inquiries) provide further details of the procedure for obtaining accounts and making inquiries. CPR Pt 25 r 25.1(1)(n) and PD 25 (accounts and inquiries) provides that the court may make an interim order for accounts to be drawn up. If the only dispute relates to the fact of the account, the court may make a summary order for accounts and inquiries (CPR Pt 24 and PD 24, para 6).

13.4.1 Payment into court

Pending the making of an account, a partner holding partnership money may be ordered to make a payment into court (*Freeman v Cox* (1878) 8 Ch D 148). It must be sufficiently probable that such a sum will be payable on the taking of an account (*Wanklyn v Wilson* (1887) 35 Ch D 180). It will not be ordered if other partners holding partnership money are not prepared to make a payment in unless the partner admits to wrongful receipt of the money (*Foster v Donald* (1820) 1 Jac & W 252; 37 ER 371) or if the partner claims that, on taking the account, an overall balance will be due to him (*Richardson v Bank of England* (1838) 4 My & Cr 165; 41 ER 65). CPR Pt 36 r 36 provides details for the making of such payments.

If the partner who has paid in to the court is sued by the partnership's creditors, he may seek a provision in the order for payment of debts to be made out of the sum paid in.

13.4.2 Disclosure of documents

As discussed in 4.4, s 24(9) of the 1890 Act entitles all partners to inspect and copy partnership books. It also provides that a partner may authorise his agent to inspect the documents, although the other partners may object to this on reasonable grounds (*Bevan v Webb* [1901] 2 Ch 59). As discussed in 4.2.1, s 28 entitles partners to receive full information about the partnership.

The CPR also provides for further information to be provided and documents to be disclosed. CPR Pt 18 and PD 18 provide that a written request for information or clarification may be sought from the other party to the proceedings, giving a reasonable time to respond, but setting a date for a response. If there is no or insufficient response, an application may be made to the court under CPR Pt 18 for further information. CPR Pt 31 r 31 provides for the disclosure of documents. In the case of a law firm, legal professional privilege may not be claimed to restrict disclosure of documents which do not relate to privileged events (*Lewthwaite v Stimson* (1966) 110 SJ 188).

In exceptional circumstances, a partner may also seek a search order (formerly known as an Anton Piller order: see *Anton Piller KG v Manufacturing Processes Ltd* [1976] Ch 55) in order to protect vital evidence from possible destruction or loss (CPR Pt 25 r 25.1(1)(h)).

13.4.3 Limitation

Actions for account cannot become time barred during the life of the partnership. However, on dissolution or expulsion, the Limitation Act 1980 applies and the action is subject to the same limitation period as governs the claim underlying the action for account. Sections 28 and 32 of the Limitation Act provide that this limitation period may be extended by fraud of the defendant partners or the disability of the claimant partner.

Where a partner negligently fails to bring an action for an account, this may indicate his acquiescence and, thus, lead the court to apply the doctrine of laches and refuse to grant the equitable remedy of an account.

13.4.4 Defences

It is a defence to an action for account that:

• a partnership does not exist;

• a settled account has been agreed already in writing and accepted by all partners (this may also operate as a partial defence where the account required covers transactions which have not been the subject of a settled account) (*Taylor v Shaw* (1824) 2 Sim & St 12; 57 ER 249);

- the underlying dispute has been settled by an arbitration award binding on the claimant partner (see, further, 7.1).

13.4.5 Judgment

The judgment will require the account to be taken of all dealings from a specified date (usually the date of the last settled account), the account calculated to be due to be certified and payment made by one party to the other in accordance with it.

13.4.6 Taking the account

At the time of writing, the Practice Direction on accounts and inquiries under CPR Pt 40 has still to be published, but, when available, it should be consulted for detailed provisions. Formerly, the position was that the account could be taken by a professional accountant or, in the High Court, by the official referee (RSC Ord 32 r 16).

The profits and losses of the partnership will be apportioned according to the partnership agreement.

13.5 Rescission of the partnership agreement

A partnership agreement may, as a contract, be rescinded on the ground that fraud or misrepresentation by one of the parties induced another partner to enter into the agreement (*Senayake v Cheng* [1966] AC 63). Section 41 of the 1890 Act provides that the partner entitled to rescind is also entitled to:

- a lien on, or right of retention of, any surplus of the partnership assets after satisfying partnership debts, in order to recover his capital;
- take the place of a partnership creditor if he has paid the creditor in respect of partnership liabilities;
- be indemnified by the party guilty of fraud or misrepresentation against the debts and liabilities of the partnership.

Such a partner is also entitled to damages for any loss sustained by him as a consequence of the fraud or fraudulent misrepresentation of his co-partners (*Redgrave v Hurd* (1881–82) 20 Ch D 1).

13.6 Action for specific performance

The remedy of specific performance of the partnership agreement will rarely be granted (*Sichel v Mosenthal* (1862) 30 Beav 371; ER 54 932). Where the partnership is at will (see 1.7.1), a partner could render such a remedy meaningless by dissolving the partnership.

13.7 Action for damages

Damages may be awarded for breach of a term of the partnership agreement.

13.8 Appointment of a receiver

Schedule 1 of the CPR re-enacts RSC Ord 30 on receivers, which now applies both to the High Court and the county court. As mentioned in 8.2.1, a receiver may be appointed on dissolution, but may also be appointed without dissolution (*Sobell v Boston* [1975] 1 WLR 1587). The following provide examples of when a receiver may be appointed:

* where the misconduct of a partner has jeopardised partnership assets and destroyed the relationship of mutual trust (*Sheppard v Oxenford* (1855) 1 K & J 491; 69 ER 552; *Harding v Glover* (1810) 18 Ves 281; 34 ER 323);

* where a partner has wrongfully excluded another partner from management (*Const v Harris* (1824) Turn & R 496; 37 ER 1191).

The courts are particularly unwilling to appoint a receiver where the partnership is a professional firm (see *Floydd v Cheney* [1970] 2 WLR 314; *Sobell v Boston* [1975] 1 WLR 1587).

13.9 Practical advice

The substantive issues of law which may bear upon disputes among partners have been discussed earlier in this book.

If an appropriate partnership agreement is drafted (see 3.1 and Appendix 4) and observed, the opportunities for dispute will be minimised. In the event that a serious dispute does arise, it is advisable to attempt to resolve the matter out of court (see 7.1 and 7.2). An adviser should be aware of potential conflicts of interest if he attempts to advise more than one party or if he has advised more than one partner in the past.

14 The Future

In addition to the probable introduction of limited liability partnerships (LLPs) (see 14.1) and multi-disciplinary partnerships (MDPs) (see 10.2) in the near future and the review of insolvency law (see Chapter 9), other aspects of partnership law may also be reformed as a result of the review currently being undertaken by the Law Commission.

14.1 Limited liability partnerships

The risks incurred by partners as a result of their unlimited liability were highlighted by the case of *ADT Ltd v BDO Binder Hamlyn* [1996] BCLC 808, in which a purchaser of a company claimed damages against the company's auditors for the negligent misrepresentation that the accounts of the company gave a true and fair representation of its financial position when, in fact, that was not the case. The High Court awarded judgment to the plaintiff for £65,000,000. The defendant's professional indemnity insurance covered only £31,000,000 and, therefore, the shortfall had to be made up by the 150 or so partners.

There are particular dangers for salaried partners and any others who are held out (and therefore potentially liable) as partners, but who receive a salary rather than a share in the profits, and who have limited or no management rights. Although such 'partners' may be indemnified by the real partners, this indemnity may be worthless if a claim against a partnership exceeds its insurance cover.

It is risks such as these which the LLP Bill (URN 99/1025) is designed to combat. Before considering the LLP Bill itself, three points of difference between the original proposals (Department of Trade and Industry, *A New Form of Business Association for the Professions*, February 1997, URN 97/579) and the LLP Bill as currently drafted should be noted. First, the proposal that every member must guarantee to contribute to a specified amount if the assets available to a liquidator are less than a specified sum related to the size of the business has been removed. Secondly, the possibility of a bond, as required for a Jersey LLP under the Limited Liability Partnership (Jersey) Law 1996, has not been pursued.

The DTI initially suggested that it would be difficult to set a specified sum which would provide a reasonable guarantee for creditors, and yet not be an unreasonable disincentive to firms, and it now also argues that limited companies offer no such protection and LLPs should therefore not be required to do so. Thirdly, as discussed at 10.1, the first draft Bill (URN 98/974) provided that LLPs must be regulated by professional bodies, and this must consist of professionals. This restriction is no longer to apply.

The LLP will be a body corporate with separate legal personality (s 1). Internal organisation is the same as that for partnership, that is to say, it is up to the partners (s 6) and it will be treated as a partnership for taxation purposes (s 10) (see Chapter 11).

14.1.1 Setting up an LLP

The LLP will be set up by registration with the Registrar of Companies. This requires submission of an incorporation document and a document stating the intended address of its registered office. Section 2 of the Bill provides that the incorporation document must contain:

- the name of the LLP (which must end with 'llp' or 'limited liability partnership');
- whether the registered office is to be situated in England and Wales, Wales or Scotland,
- the name and address of the members.

14.1.2 Liability of the members

Members are agents of the LLP but, unlike partners, are not agents of each other. The LLP will therefore be liable for acts of its members in the ordinary course of business which are authorised (s 7) but the members will not be personally liable. The exceptions to this are as follows:

- a member who is guilty of wrongdoing under the general law will be personally liable for his acts;
- the 'clawback' (see 14.1.3) may apply if the LLP is insolvent;
- a member who is guilty of fraudulent or wrongful trading (see 9.3.5) may be ordered to contribute to the assets of an insolvent LLP.

It should also be noted that the assets of the LLP may be reduced by the wrongful act of a particular member giving rise to a claim against those assets. This would also bring closer the likelihood of insolvency and therefore the 'clawback' (see 14.1.3) may be brought nearer.

14.1.3 The clawback

Schedule 3 of the regulations, on the application of the IA 1986, inserts a new s 214A which provides that a liquidator of an LLP may clawback drawings made by a member of the LLP within two years prior to the winding up where that member knew, or had reasonable grounds for believing, that the LLP was insolvent or would be made insolvent by the withdrawal taken together with other withdrawals made or contemplated by other members at that time.

14.1.4 Access to the LLP

The Bill as originally drafted envisaged that LLPs would be regulated by a regulatory body recognised for the purpose by the Secretary of State, and would therefore be limited to professional firms. However, as explained at 14.1, the Government has now agreed that the LLP vehicle is to be available to two or more persons carrying on any trade or profession.

14.1.5 Other safeguards for creditors

The regulations provide that creditors of LLPs will have the statutory safeguards (with appropriate modifications) of wrongful and fraudulent trading (ss 213 and 214 of the IA 1986), investigations (ss 431–34, 436–39, 441 and 447–51 of the Companies Act 1985) and the Company Directors Disqualification Act 1986 (CDDA).

Disclosure of financial information equivalent to that disclosed by companies will also be required. This means that audited accounts giving details of the capital contributions of the partners and the profits and losses of the partnership must be filed and will be available for public inspection. In addition, the regulations provide that where profits exceed £200,000 the amount to which the member with the largest profit share is entitled must be disclosed (Schedule 1 to the regulations).

14.2 Law Commission review

The Law Commission is currently working on a number of possible reforms to the 1890 Act, and is then due to consider the Limited Partnerships Act 1907.

The key areas under review include:

• whether partnerships should be given independent legal personality (which would enable them to contract in their own name and own property, but would not affect the position regarding ownership of land) (see 2.3 and 3.4.3);

- whether automatic dissolution in the event of the retirement, death or bankruptcy of a partner is still appropriate (see 8.1.1).

The review also includes consideration of:

- whether the limit on the number of partners, and the exceptions to this, should remain (see 1.5);

- the possible introduction of a form of perpetual succession for partnerships (see 2.3);

- the possible introduction of a statutory power of expulsion (see 7.4);

- the possible introduction of a model partnership agreement, either in the form of a revised Act, or a statutory instrument (which would be easier to amend);

- the simplification of solvent dissolution;

- the introduction of provisions to ascertain the amount of a partner's share in the partnership; whether it is appropriate for statute to provide a mechanism for the valuation of a partner's share; and what any such mechanism should be. The chief difficulty identified by the Law Commission in this area is that there is no uniform approach to accounting in partnerships;

- the treatment of goodwill on dissolution (see 3.4.6 and 8.3);

- whether statute should provide default provisions in respect of time devoted to business;

- appropriate remedies for breach of the partnership agreement;

- registration of partnerships;

- clarification of the duty of good faith.

The Law Commission has not yet published its recommendations.

14.3 Practical advice

The probable introduction of LLPs in the near future could provide a genuine alternative to existing partnerships, and partners will need detailed advice on the advantages and disadvantages. Such advice will also depend on the changes made to partnership law as a result of the Law Commission review.

15 Further Reading

There are relatively few publications of any sort devoted wholly or mainly to partnership law, although many journals and books cover this topic within the broader heading of business or commercial law. The following partnership law texts, therefore, have few competitors.

Partnership law texts

I'Anson Banks (ed), *Lindley and Banks on Partnership*, 17th edn, 1995, Sweet and Maxwell

A comprehensive text which covers all aspects of partnership law, including taxation. It also reproduces the key statutes and statutory instruments.

Blackett-Ord, *Partnership*, 1997, Butterworths

Similar in content and detail to *Lindley and Banks*, but also covers litigation (although it predates the introduction of the Civil Procedure Rules) and provides two sample partnership agreements.

Morse, *Partnership Law*, 4th edn, 1998, Blackstone

The best known of the shorter partnership books. It is both readable and authoritative.

Prime and Scanlon, *The Law of Partnership*, 1995, Butterworths

Less well known than Morse, this book has the advantage of covering partnership taxation and issues of litigation before the introduction of the CPR.

Atkin's Court Forms, Vols 30 (partnership actions) and 30(1) (partnership insolvency), Butterworths

Other relevant titles

Clarke, *Business Entities*, 1996, Sweet & Maxwell

Contains a summary of the law relating to partnerships, including tax, a solicitor's checklist and a sample partnership agreement. It also provides an introduction to company law.

Hewitt, *Joint Ventures*, 1977, FT Law and Tax/Pearson

Considers all legal aspects of joint ventures, including the possible use of a partnership as the vehicle for the joint venture.

Mayson, *Making Sense of Law Firm Management*, 1997, Blackstone

Considers both theoretical and practical issues arising in the context of the management of a particular type of partnership: the law firm.

Davey, Parry–Wingfield and Clarke, *Ray: Partnership Taxation*, 1996, Butterworths Tolley

Updated in 1998, this looseleaf volume contains a comprehensive explanation of all aspects of partnership taxation, including issues arising on incorporation and joint ventures.

Eastaway and Gilligan, *Tax and Financial Planning for Professional Partnerships*, 3rd edn, 1996, Butterworths

Covers partnership taxation and other financial issues, such as insurance and pensions, as they relate to professional firms. There are a considerable number of worked examples.

Whitehouse, *Revenue Law: Principles and Practice*, 16th edn, 1998, Butterworths

Contains details of the law applicable to the taxation of partnerships, with worked examples.

Plant (ed), *Blackstone's Guide to the Civil Procedure Rules*, 1999, Blackstone

A useful practitioner's guide to the new court rules and Practice Directions, with helpful commentary, copies of court forms and the text of the rules and Practice Directions.

Grainger and Fealy, *An Introduction to the New Civil Procedure Rules*, 1999, Cavendish Publishing

A useful guide to the rules for the busy practitioner, with a concise commentary, the text of the rules and Practice Directions interleaved.

Law reports

There are no reports devoted specifically to partnership law, but general series such as the All England Law Reports and the Weekly Law Reports report most partnership law cases, although many cases predate these reports and can only be found in the English Reports.

http://www.parliament.the-stationery-office.co.uk/pa/ld/djudinf.htm

House of Lords judgments delivered since 14 November 1996 can be found at this website within two hours of their delivery.

Butterworths Company Law Cases (BCLC)

This series commenced in 1983. Issued monthly, it includes, despite the title, the text of some leading cases on partnership law.

Journals

Journal of Business Law (JBL), Sweet & Maxwell

Bi-monthly journal with occasional articles and notes on partnership law.

The Company Lawyer (Co Law), Sweet & Maxwell

16 Useful Sources of Information

The London Gazette
PO Box 7923
London SE1 5ZH
Tel: 020 7394 4580
Fax: 020 7394 4581

The Edinburgh Gazette
21 South Gyle Crescent
Edinburgh EH12 9EB
Tel: 0131 479 3143
Fax: 0131 479 3311

The Belfast Gazette
IDB House
64 Chichester Street
Belfast BT1 4PS
Tel: 028 895135
Fax: 028 895152

For registration of limited partnerships or companies and explanatory notes

The Registrar of Limited Partnerships or of Companies at one of the following addresses (according to the part of the UK in which the business is to have its principal place of business):

Companies House

Crown Way

Maindy

Cardiff CF4 3UZ

Tel: 029 388 588

Fax: 029 380 900

Companies House

55–71 City Road

London EC1Y 1BB

Tel: 020 7253 9393

Fax: 020 7608 0435

Companies House

37 Castle Terrace

Edinburgh EH1 2EB

Tel: 0131 535 5800

Fax: 0131 535 5820

Department of Commerce

64 Chichester Street

Belfast BT1 4JX

Tel: 028 234488

Fax: 028 544888

For inspection of documents relating to limited partnerships or companies

Companies House at any of the above addresses and at:

Companies House
25 Queen Street
Leeds LS1 2TW
Tel: 0113 233 8338
Fax: 0113 233 8335

Companies House
75 Mosley Street
Manchester M2 2HR
Tel: 0161 236 7500
Fax: 0161 237 5228

Companies House
Birmingham Central Library
Chamberlain Square
Birmingham B3 3HQ
Tel: 0121 233 9047
Fax: 0121 233 9052

Companies House
21 West George Street
Glasgow G2 1BQ
Tel: 0141 221 5513
Fax: 0141 225 2870

Regarding alternative dispute resolution

Centre for Alternative Dispute Resolution (CEDR)

Princes House

95 Gresham Street

London EC2V 7NA

Tel: 020 7600 0500

Fax: 020 7600 0501

Website http://www.cedr.co.uk/

ADR Group

Equity and Law Building

36–38 Baldwin Street

Bristol BS1 1NR

Tel: 0117 925 2090

Fax: 0117 929 4429

Website http://www.adrgroup.co.uk/

Regarding arbitration

Chartered Institute of Arbitrators

24 Angel Gate

City Road

London EC1V 2RS

Tel: 020 7837 4483

Fax: 020 7837 4185

Website http://www.arbitrators.org/

Regarding the LLP Bill

Department of Trade and Industry

Company and Investments Law Directorate

1 Victoria Street

London SW1H 0ET

Tel: 020 7215 0229

Fax: 0207215 0235

Website http://www.dti.gov.uk/cld/llpbill/index.htm

Regarding the Law Commission's review of partnership law

The Law Commission

Conquest House

37–38 John Street

Theobalds Road

London WC1N 2BQ

Tel: 020 7453 1220

Fax: 020 7453 1297

Website http://www.open.gov.uk/lawcomm/homepage.htm

Appendix 1: Partnership Act 1890

Name of partnership

1 Definition of partnership

(1) Partnership is the relation which subsists between persons carrying on a business in common with a view of profit.

(2) But the relation between members of any company or association which is:

(a) registered as a company under the Companies Act 1862 or any other Act of Parliament for the time being in force and relating to the registration of joint stock companies; or

(b) formed or incorporated by or in pursuance of any other Act of Parliament or letters patent or royal charter; or

(c) a company engaged in working mines within and subject to the jurisdiction of the Stannaries

is not a partnership within the meaning of this Act.

2 Rules for determining existence of partnership

In determining whether a partnership does or does not exist, regard shall be had to the following rules:

(1) Joint tenancy, tenancy in common, joint property, common property, or part ownership does not of itself create a partnership as to anything so held or owned, whether the tenants or owners do or do not share any profits made by the use thereof.

(2)   The sharing of gross returns does not of itself create a partnership, whether the persons sharing such returns have or have not a joint or common right or interest in any property from which or from the use of which the returns are derived.

(3)   The receipt by a person of a share of the profits of a business is prima facie evidence that he is a partner in the business, but the receipt of such a share, or of a payment contingent on or varying with the profits of a business, does not of itself make him a partner in the business; and in particular–

(a)   the receipt by a person of a debt or other liquidated amount by instalments or otherwise out of the accruing profits of a business does not of itself make him a partner in the business or liable as such,

(b)   a contract for the remuneration of a servant or agent of a person engaged in a business by a share of the profits of the business does not of itself make the servant or agent a partner in the business or liable as such,

(c)   a person being the widow or child of a deceased partner, and receiving by way of annuity a portion of the profits made in the business in which the deceased person was a partner, is not by reason only of such receipt a partner in the business or liable as such,

(d)   the advance of money by way of loan to a person engaged or about to engage in any business on a contract with that person that the lender shall receive a rate of interest varying with the profits, or shall receive a share of the profits arising from carrying on the business, does not of itself make the lender a partner with the person or persons carrying on the business or liable as such. Provided that the contract is in writing, and signed by or on behalf of all the parties thereto,

(e)   a person receiving by way of annuity or otherwise a portion of the profits of a business in consideration of the sale by him of the goodwill of the business is not by reason only of such receipt a partner in the business or liable as such.

3   Postponement of rights of person lending or selling in consideration of share of profits in case of insolvency

In the event of any person to whom money has been advanced by way of loan upon such a contract as is mentioned in the last foregoing section, or of any buyer of goodwill in consideration of a share of the profits of the business, being adjudged a bankrupt, entering into an arrangement to pay his creditors less than [100p] in the pound, or dying in insolvent circumstances, the lender of the loan shall not be entitled to recover anything in respect of his loan, and the seller of the goodwill shall not be entitled to recover anything in respect of the share of profits contracted for, until the claims of the other creditors of the borrower or buyer for valuable consideration in money or money's worth have been satisfied.

4   Meaning of firm

(1)   Persons who have entered into partnership with one another are for the purposes of this Act called collectively a 'firm', and the name under which their business is carried on is called the 'firm-name'.

(2)   In Scotland a firm is a legal person distinct from the partners of whom it is composed, but an individual partner may be charged on a decree or diligence directed against the firm, and on payment of the debts is entitled to relief *pro rata* from the firm and its other members.

Relations of partners to persons dealing with them

5   Power of partner to bind the firm

Every partner is an agent of the firm and his other partners for the purpose of the business of the partnership; and the acts of every partner who does any act for carrying on in the usual way business of the kind carried on by the firm of which he is a member bind the firm and his partners, unless the partner so acting has in fact no authority to act for the firm in the particular matter, and the person with whom he is dealing either knows that he has no authority, or does not know or believe him to be a partner.

6   Partners bound by acts on behalf of firm

An act or instrument relating to the business of the firm done or executed in the firm-name or in any other manner showing an intention to bind the firm, by any person thereto authorised, whether a partner or not, is binding on the firm and all the partners.

Provided that this section shall not affect any general rule of law relating to the execution of deeds or negotiable instruments.

7   Partner using credit of firm for private purposes

Where one partner pledges the credit of the firm for a purpose apparently not connected with the firm's ordinary course of business, the firm is not bound, unless he is in fact specially authorised by the other partners; but this section does not affect any personal liability incurred by an individual partner.

8   Effect of notice that firm will not be bound by acts of partner

If it has been agreed between the partners that any restriction shall be placed on the power of any one or more of them to bind the firm, no act done in contravention of the agreement is binding on the firm with respect to persons having notice of the agreement.

9   Liability of partners

Every partner in a firm is liable jointly with the other partners, and in Scotland severally also, for all debts and obligations of the firm incurred while he is a partner; and after his death his estate is also severally liable in a due course of administration for such debts and obligations, so far as they remain unsatisfied, but subject in England or Ireland to the prior payment of his separate debts.

10   Liability of the firm for wrongs

Where, by any wrongful act or omission of any partner acting in the ordinary course of the business of the firm, or with the authority of his co-partners, loss or injury is caused to any person not being a partner in the firm, or any penalty is incurred, the firm is liable therefore to the same extent as the partner so acting or omitting to act.

11 Misapplication of money or property received for or in custody of the firm

In the following cases; namely–

(a) where one partner acting within the scope of his apparent authority receives the money or property of a third person and misapplies it; and

(b) where a firm in the course of its business receives money or property of a third person, and the money or property so received is misapplied by one or more of the partners while it is in the custody of the firm;

the firm is liable to make good the loss.

12 Liability for wrongs joint and several

Every partner is liable jointly with his co-partners and also severally for everything for which the firm while he is a partner therein becomes liable under either of the two last preceding sections.

13 Improper employment of trust property for partnership purposes

If a partner, being a trustee, improperly employs trust property in the business or on the account of the partnership, no other partner is liable for the trust-property to the persons beneficially interested therein:

Provided as follows–

(1) this section shall not affect any liability incurred by any partner by reason of his having notice of a breach of trust; and

(2) nothing in this section shall prevent trust money from being followed and recovered from the firm if still in its possession or under its control.

14 Persons liable by 'holding out'

(1) Every one who by words spoken or written or by conduct represents himself, or who knowingly suffers himself to be represented, as a partner in a particular firm, is liable as a partner to any one who has on the faith of any such representation given credit to the firm, whether the representation has or has not been made or communicated to the person so giving credit by or with

the knowledge of the apparent partner making the representation or suffering it to be made.

(2)   Provided that where after a partner's death the partnership business is continued in the old firm's name, the continued use of that name or of the deceased partner's name as part thereof shall not of itself make his executors or administrators estate or effects liable for any partnership debts contracted after his death.

15   Admissions and representations of partners

An admission or representation made by any partner concerning the partnership affairs, and in the ordinary course of its business is evidence against the firm.

16   Notice to acting partner to be notice to the firm

Notice to any partner who habitually acts in the partnership business of any matter relating to partnership affairs operates as notice to the firm, except in the case of a fraud on the firm committed by or with the consent of that partner.

17   Liabilities of incoming and outgoing partners

(1)   A person who is admitted as a partner into an existing firm does not thereby become liable to the creditors of the firm for anything done before he became a partner.

(2)   A partner who retires from a firm does not thereby cease to be liable for partnership debts or obligations incurred before his retirement.

(3)   A retiring partner may be discharged from any existing liabilities, by an agreement to that effect between himself and the members of the firm as newly constituted and the creditors, and this agreement may be either express or inferred as a fact from the course of dealing between the creditors and the firm as newly constituted.

18   Revocation of continuing guarantee by change in firm

A continuing guarantee or cautionary obligation given either to a firm or to a third person in respect of the transactions of a firm is, in the absence of agreement to the contrary, revoked as to future transactions by any change in the constitution of the firm to which, or of the firm in respect of the transactions of which, the guarantee of obligation was given.

Relations of partners to one another

19   Variation by consent of terms of partnership

The mutual rights and duties of partners, whether ascertained by agreement or defined by this Act, may be varied by the consent of all the partners, and such consent may be either express or inferred from a course of dealing.

20   Partnership property

(1)   All property and rights and interests in property originally brought into the partnership stock or acquired, whether by purchase or otherwise, on account of the firm, or for the purposes and in the course of the partnership business, are called in this Act partnership property, and must be held and applied by the partners exclusively for the purposes of the partnership and in accordance with the partnership agreement.

(2)   Provided that the legal estate or interest in any land, or in Scotland, the title to and interest in any heritable estate, which belongs to the partnership shall devolve according to the nature and tenure thereof, and the general rules of law thereto applicable, but in trust, so far as necessary, for the persons beneficially interested in the land under this section.

(3)   Where co-owners of an estate or interest in any land, or in Scotland of any heritable estate, not being itself partnership property, are partners as to profits made by the use of that land or estate and purchase other land or estate out of the profits to be used in like manner, the land or estate so purchased belongs to them, in the absence of an agreement to the contrary, not as partners, but as co-owners for the same respective estates and interests as are held by them in the land or estate mentioned at the date of the purchase.

21 Property bought with partnership money

Unless the contrary intention appears, property bought with money belonging to the firm is deemed to have been bought on account of the firm.

22 Conversion into personal estate of land held as partnership property

Where land or any heritable interest therein has become partnership property, it shall, unless the contrary intention appears, be treated as between the partners (including the representatives of a decreased partner) and also as between the heirs of a deceased partner and his executors or administrators, as personal or moveable and not real or heritable estate.

23 Procedure against partnership property for a partner's separate judgment debt

(1)   A writ of execution shall not issue against any partnership property except on a judgment against the firm.

(2)   The High Court, or a judge thereof, or a county court, may on the application by summons of any judgment creditor of a partner, make an order charging that partner's interest in the partnership property and profits with payment of the amount of the judgment debt and interest thereon, and may by the same or a subsequent order appoint a receiver of that partner's share of profits (whether already declared or accruing), and of any other money which may be coming to him in respect of the partnership, and direct all accounts and inquiries and give all other orders and directions which might have been directed or given if the charge had been made in favour of the judgment creditor by the partner, or which the circumstances of the case may require.

(3)   The other partner or partners shall be at liberty at any time to redeem the interest charged, or in case of a sale being directed, to purchase the same.

(4)   This section shall apply in the case of a cost-book company as if the company were a partnership within the meaning of this Act.

(5)   This section shall not apply to Scotland.

24   Rules as to interests and duties of partners subject to special agreement

The interests of partners in the partnership property and their rights and duties in relation to the partnership shall be determined, subject to any agreement express or implied between the partners, by the following rules:

(1)   All the partners are entitled to share equally in the capital and profits of the business, and must contribute equally towards the losses whether of capital or otherwise sustained by the firm.

(2)   The firm must indemnify every partner in respect of payments made and personal liabilities incurred by him—

(a)   in the ordinary and proper conduct of the business of the firm; or,

(b)   in or about anything necessarily done for the preservation of the business or property of the firm.

(3)   A partner making, for the purpose of the partnership, any actual payment or advance beyond the amount of capital which he has agreed to subscribe, is entitled to interest at the rate of 5% per annum from the date of the payment or advance.

(4)   A partner is not entitled, before the ascertainment of profits, to interest on the capital subscribed by him.

(5)   Every partner may take part in the management of the partnership business.

(6)   No partner shall be entitled to remuneration for acting in the partnership business.

(7)   No person may be introduced as a partner without the consent of all existing partners.

(8)   Any difference arising as to ordinary matters connected with the partnership business may be decided by a majority of the partners, but no change may be made in the nature of the partnership business without the consent of all existing partners.

(9)   The partnership books are to be kept at the place of business of the partnership (or the principal place, if there is more than one) and every partner may, when he thinks fit, have access to and inspect and copy any of them.

25 Expulsion of partner

No majority of the partners can expel any partner unless a power to do so has been conferred by express agreement between the partners.

26 Retirement from partnership at will

(1) Where no fixed term has been agreed upon for the duration of the partnership, any partner may determine the partnership at any time on giving notice of his intention so to do to all the other partners.

(2) Where the partnership has originally been constituted by deed, a notice in writing, signed by the partner giving it, shall be sufficient for this purpose.

27 Where partnership for term is continued over, continuance on old terms presumed

(1) Where a partnership entered into for a fixed term is continued after the term has expired, and without any express new agreement, the rights and duties of the partners remain the same as they were at the expiration of the term, so far as is consistent with the incidents of a partnership at will.

(2) A continuance of the business by the partners or such of them as habitually acted therein during the term, without any settlement or liquidation of the partnership affairs is presumed to be a continuance of the partnership.

28 Duty of partners to render accounts etc

Partners are bound to render true accounts and full information of all things affecting the partnership to any partner or his legal representatives.

29 Accountability of partners for private profits

(1) Every partner must account to the firm for any benefit derived by him without the consent of the other partners from any transaction concerning the partnership, or from any use by him of the partnership property name or business connexion.

(2) This section applies also to transactions undertaken after a partnership has been dissolved by the death of a partner, and

before the affairs thereof have been completely wound up, either by any surviving partner or by the representatives of the deceased partner.

30   Duty of partner not to compete with firm

If a partner, without the consent of the other partners, carries on any business of the same nature as and competing with that of the firm, he must account for and pay over to the firm all profits made by him in that business.

31   Rights of assignee of share in partnership

(1)   An assignment by any partner of his share in the partnership, either absolute or by way of mortgage or redeemable charge, does not, as against the other partners, entitle the assignee, during the continuance of the partnership, to interfere in the management or administration of the partnership business or affairs, or to require any accounts of the partnership transactions, or to inspect the partnership books, but entitles the assignee only to receive the share of profits to which the assigning partner would otherwise be entitled and the assignee must accept the account of profits agreed to by the partners.

(2)   In case of a dissolution of the partnership, whether as respects all the partners or as respects the assigning partner, the assignee is entitled to receive the share of the partnership assets to which the assigning partner is entitled as between himself and the other partners, and, for the purpose of ascertaining that share, to an account as from the date of the dissolution.

Dissolution of partnership, and its consequences

32   Dissolution by expiration or notice

Subject to any agreement between the partners, a partnership is dissolved–

(a)   if entered into for a fixed term, by the expiration of that term,

(b)   if entered into for a single adventure or undertaking, by the termination of that adventure or undertaking,

(c)   if entered into for an undefined time, by any partner giving notice to the other or others of his intention to dissolve the partnership.

In the last-mentioned case the partnership is dissolved as from the date mentioned in the notice as the date of dissolution, or if no date is so mentioned, as from the date of the communication of the notice.

33   Dissolution by bankruptcy, death or charge

(1)   Subject to any agreement between the partners, every partnership is dissolved as regards all the partners by the death or bankruptcy of any partner.

(2)   A partnership may, at the option of the other partners, be dissolved if any partner suffers his share of the partnership property to be charged under this Act for his separate debt.

34   Dissolution by illegality of partnership

A partnership is in every case dissolved by the happening of any event which makes it unlawful for the business of the firm to be carried on or for the members of the firm to carry it on in partnership.

35   Dissolution by the Court

On application by a partner, the Court may decree a dissolution of the partnership in any of the following cases:

(a)   when a partner, other than the partner suing, becomes in any other way permanently incapable of performing his part of the partnership contract,

(b)   when a partner, other than the partner suing, has been guilty of such conduct as, in the opinion of the Court, regard being had to the nature of the business, is calculated to prejudicially affect the carrying on of the business,

(c)   when a partner, other than the partner suing, wilfully or persistently commits a breach of the partnership agreement, or otherwise so conducts himself in matters relating to the partnership business that it is not reasonably practicable for the other partner or partners to carry on the business in partnership with him,

(d)   when the business of the partnership can only be carried on at a loss,

(e)   whenever in any case circumstances have arisen which, in the opinion of the Court, render it just and equitable that the partnership be dissolved.

36   Rights of persons dealing with firm against apparent members of firm

(1)   Where a person deals with a firm after a change in its constitution he is entitled to treat all apparent members of the old firm as still being members of the firm until he has notice of the change.

(2)   An advertisement in the *London Gazette* as to a firm whose principal place of business is in England or Wales, in the *Edinburgh Gazette* as to a firm whose principal place of business is in Scotland, and in the [*Belfast*] *Gazette* as to a firm whose principal place of business is in [Northern] Ireland, shall be notice as to persons who had no dealing with the firm before the date of the dissolution or change so advertised.

(3)   The estate of a partner who dies, or who becomes bankrupt, or of a partner who, not having been known to the person dealing with the firm to be a partner, retires from the firm, is not liable for partnership debts contracted after the date of the death, bankruptcy, or retirement respectively.

37   Right of partners to notify dissolution

On the dissolution of a partnership or retirement of a partner any partner may publicly notify the same, and may require the other partner or partners to concur for that purpose in all necessary or proper acts, if any, which cannot be done without his or their concurrence.

38   Continuing authority of partners for purposes of winding up

After the dissolution of a partnership the authority of each partner to bind the firm, and the other rights and obligations of the partners, continue notwithstanding the dissolution so far as may be necessary to wind up the affairs of the partnership, and to complete transactions begun but unfinished at the time of the dissolution, but not otherwise.

Provided that the firm is in no case bound by the acts of a partner who has become bankrupt; but this proviso does not affect the liability of any person who has after the bankruptcy represented himself or knowingly suffered himself to be represented as a partner of the bankrupt.

39   Rights of partners as to application of partnership property

On the dissolution of a partnership every partner is entitled, as against the other partners in the firm, and all persons claiming through them in respect of their interests as partners, to have the property of the partnership applied in payment of the debts and liabilities of the firm, and to have the surplus assets after such payment applied in payment of what may be due to the partners respectively after deducting what may be due from them as partners to the firm; and for that purpose any partner or his representatives may on the termination of the partnership apply to the Court to wind up the business and affairs of the firm.

40   Apportionment of premium where partnership prematurely dissolved

Where one partner has paid a premium to another on entering into a partnership for a fixed term and the partnership is dissolved before the expiration of that term otherwise than by the death of a partner the Court may order the repayment of the premium, or of such part thereof as it thinks just, having regard to the terms of the partnership contract and to the length of time during which the partnership has continued; unless—

(a)   the dissolution is, in the judgment of the Court, wholly or chiefly due to the misconduct of the partner who paid the premium, or

(b)   the partnership has been dissolved by an agreement containing no provision for a return of any part of the premium.

41   Rights where partnership dissolved for fraud or misrepresentation

Where a partnership contract is rescinded on the ground of the fraud or misrepresentation of one of the parties thereto, the party entitled to rescind it, without prejudice to any other right, is entitled—

(a)   to a lien on, or right of retention of, the surplus of the partnership assets, after satisfying the partnership liabilities, for any sum of money paid by him for the purchase of a share in the partnership and for any capital contributed by him, and is

(b)   to stand in the place of the creditors of the firm for any payments made by him in respect of the partnership liabilities, and

(c)   to be indemnified by the person guilty of the fraud or making the representation against all the debts and liabilities of the firm.

42   Right of outgoing partner in certain cases to share profits made after dissolution

(1)   Where any member of a firm has died or otherwise ceased to be a partner, and the surviving or continuing partners carry on the business of the firm with its capital or assets without any final settlement of accounts as between the firm and the outgoing partner or his estate, then, in the absence of any agreement to the contrary, the outgoing partner or his estate is entitled at the option of himself or his representatives to such share of the profits made since the dissolution as the Court may find to be attributable to the use of his share of the partnership assets, or to interest at the rate of 5% per annum on the amount of his share of the partnership assets.

(2)   Provided that where by the partnership contract an option is given to surviving or continuing partners to purchase the interest of a deceased or outgoing partner, and that option is duly exercised, the estate of the deceased partner, or the outgoing partner or his estate, as the case may be, is not entitled to any further or other share of profits; but if any partner assuming to act in exercise of the option does not in all material respects comply with the terms thereof, he is liable to account under the foregoing provisions of this section.

43   Retiring or deceased partner's share to be a debt

Subject to any agreement between the partners, the amount due from surviving or continuing partners to an outgoing partner or the representatives of a deceased partner in respect of the outgoing or deceased partner's share is a debt accruing at the date of the dissolution or death.

44   Rule for distribution of assets on final settlement of accounts

In settling accounts between the partners after a dissolution of partnership, the following rules shall, subject to any agreement, be observed:

(a)   losses, including losses and deficiencies of capital, shall be paid first out of profits, next out of capital, and, lastly, if necessary, by the partners individually in the proportion in which they were entitled to share profit:

(b)   the assets of the firm including the sums, if any, contributed by the partners to make up losses or deficiencies of capital, shall be applied in the following manner and order:

1.   in paying the debts and liabilities of the firm to persons who are not partners therein,

2.   in paying to each partner rateably what is due from the firm to him for advances as distinguished from capital,

3.   in paying to each partner rateably what is due from the firm to him in respect of capital,

4.   the ultimate residue, if any, shall be divided among the partners in the proportion in which profits are divisible.

Supplemental

45   Definitions of 'court' and 'business'

In this Act, unless the contrary intention appears–

The expression 'court' includes every court and judge having jurisdiction in the case:

the expression 'business' includes every trade, occupation, or profession.

46   Saving for rules of equity and common law

The rules of equity and of common law applicable to partnership shall continue in force except so far as they are inconsistent with the express provisions of this Act.

47   Provision as to bankruptcy in Scotland

(1)   In the application of this Act to Scotland the bankruptcy of a firm or of an individual shall mean sequestration under the Bankruptcy (Scotland) Acts, and also in the case of an individual the issue against him of a decree of *cessio bonorum*.

(2)   Nothing in this Act shall alter the rules of the law of Scotland relating to the bankruptcy of a firm or of the individual partners thereof.

[Sections 48 and 49 repealed]

50   Short title

This Act may be cited as the Partnership Act, 1890.

Appendix 2: Limited Partnerships Act 1907

1 Short title

This Act may be cited for all purposes as the Limited Partnerships Act 1907.

[Section 2 repealed]

3 Interpretation of terms

In the construction of this Act the following words and expressions shall have the meanings respectively assigned to them in this section, unless there be something in the subject or context repugnant to such construction–

'Firm', 'firm name' and 'business' have the same meanings as in the Partnership Act 1890:

'General partner' shall mean any partner who is not a limited partner as defined by this Act.

4 Definition and constitution of limited partnership

(1) Limited partnerships may be formed in the manner and subject to the conditions by this Act provided.

(2) A limited partnership shall not consist of more than 20 persons, and must consist of one or more persons called general partners, who shall be liable for all debts and obligations of the firm, and one or more persons to be called limited partners, who shall at the time of entering into such partnership contribute, thereto a

sum or sums as capital or property valued at a stated amount, and who shall not be liable for the debts or obligations of the firm beyond the amount so contributed.

(3)   A limited partner shall not during the continuance of the partnership, either directly or indirectly, draw out or receive back any part of his contribution, and if he does so draw out or receive back such part shall be liable for the debts and obligations of the firm up to the amount so drawn out or received back.

(4)   A body corporate may be a limited partner.

5   Registration of limited partnership required

Every limited partnership must be registered as such in accordance with the provisions of this Act, or in default thereof it shall be deemed to be a general partnership, and every limited partner shall be deemed to be a general partner.

6   Modification of general law in case of limited partnerships

(1)   A limited partner shall not take part in the management of the partnership business, and shall not have power to bind the firm:

Provided that a limited partner may, by himself or his agent, at any time inspect the books of the firm and examine into the state and prospects of the partnership business, and may advise with the partners thereon.

If a limited partner takes part in the management of the partnership business he shall be liable for all debts and obligations of the firm incurred while he so takes part in the management as though he were a general partner.

(2)   A limited partnership shall not be dissolved by the death or bankruptcy of a limited partner, and the lunacy of a limited partner shall not be a ground for dissolution of the partnership by the court unless the lunatic's share cannot be otherwise ascertained and realised.

(3)   In the event of the dissolution of a limited partnership its affairs shall be wound up by the general partners unless the court otherwise orders.

(4)   [Repealed]

(5)   Subject to any agreement expressed or implied between the partners—

    (a)   any difference arising as to ordinary matters connected with the partnership business may be decided by a majority of the general partners;

    (b)   a limited partner may, with the consent of the general partners, assign his share in the partnership, and upon such an assignment the assignee shall become a limited partner with all the rights of the assignor;

    (c)   the other partners shall not be entitled to dissolve the partnership by reason of any limited partner suffering his share to be charged for his separate debt;

    (d)   a person may be introduced as a partner without the consent of the existing limited partners;

    (e)   a limited partner shall not be entitled to dissolve the partnership by notice.

7   Law as to private partnerships to apply where not excluded by this Act

Subject to the provisions of this Act, the Partnership Act 1890 and the rules of equity and of common law applicable to partnerships, except so far as they are inconsistent with the express provisions of the last-mentioned Act, shall apply to limited partnerships.

8   Manner and particulars of registration

The registration of a limited partnership shall be effected by sending by post or delivering to the registrar at the register office in that part of the United Kingdom in which the principal place of business of the limited partnership is situated or proposed to be situated a statement signed by the partners containing the following particulars:

    (a)   the firm name;

    (b)   the general nature of the business;

    (c)   the principal place of business;

    (d)   the full name of each of the partners;

    (e)   the term, if any, for which the partnership is entered into and the date of its commencement;

(f)   a statement that the partnership is limited, and the description of every limited partner as such;

(g)   the sum contributed by each limited partner and whether paid in cash or how otherwise.

9   Registration of changes in partnerships

(1)   If during the continuance of a limited partnership any change is made or occurs in–

(a)   the firm name;

(b)   the general nature of the business;

(c)   the principal place of business;

(d)   the partners or the name of any partner;

(e)   the term or character of the partnership;

(f)   the sum contributed by any limited partner;

(g)   the liability of any partner by reason of his becoming a limited instead of a general partner or a general instead of a limited partner;

a statement, signed by the firm, specifying the nature of the change shall within seven days be sent by post or delivered to the registrar at the register office in that part of the United Kingdom in which the partnership is registered.

(2)   If default is made in compliance with the requirements of this section each of the general partners shall, on conviction under the Summary Jurisdiction Acts, be liable to a fine not exceeding one pound for each day during which the default continues.

10   Advertisement in *Gazette* of statement of general partner becoming a limited partner and of assignment of share of limited partner

(1)   Notice of any arrangement or transaction under which any person will cease to be a general partner in any firm, and will become a limited partner in that firm, or under which the share of a limited partner in a firm will be assigned to any person, shall be

forthwith advertised in the *Gazette*, and until notice of the arrangement or transaction is so advertised the arrangement or transaction shall, for the purposes of this Act, be deemed to be of no effect.

(2) For the purposes of this section, the expression the '*Gazette*' means–

In the case of a limited partnership registered in England, the *London Gazette*.

In the case of a limited partnership registered in Scotland, the *Edinburgh Gazette*.

In the case of a limited partnership registered in [Northern] Ireland, the [*Belfast*] *Gazette*.

[Sections 11 and 12 repealed]

13   Registrar to file statement and issue certificate of registration

On receiving any statement made in pursuance of this Act the registrar shall cause the same to be filed, and he shall send by post to the firm from whom such statement shall have been received a certificate of the registration thereof.

14   Register and index to be kept

At each of the register offices herein after referred to the registrar shall keep, in proper books to be provided for the purpose, a register and an index of all the limited partnerships registered as aforesaid, and of all the statements registered in relation to such partnerships.

15   Registrar of joint stock companies to be registrar under Act

The registrar of joint stock companies shall be the registrar of limited partnerships, and the several offices for the registration of joint stock companies in London, Edinburgh and [Belfast] shall be the offices for the registration of limited partnerships carrying on business within those parts of the United Kingdom in which they are respectively situated.

16   Inspection of statements registered

(1)   Any person may inspect the statements filed by the registrar in the register offices aforesaid, and there shall be paid for such inspection such fees as may be appointed by the Board of Trade, not exceeding [5p] for each inspection; and any person may require a certificate of the registration of any limited partnership, or a copy of or extract from any registered statement, to be certified by the registrar, and there shall be paid for such certificate of registration, certified copy, or extract such fees as the Board of Trade may appoint, not exceeding [10p] for the certificate of registration and not exceeding [2p] for each folio of 72 words, or in Scotland for each sheet of 200 words.

(2)   A certificate of registration or a copy of or extract from any statement registered under this Act, if duly certified to be a true copy under the hand of the registrar or one of the assistant registrars (whom it shall not be necessary to prove to be the registrar or assistant registrar), shall, in all legal proceedings, civil or criminal, and in all cases whatsoever be received in evidence.

17   Power to Board of Trade to make rules

The Board of Trade may make rules (but as to fees with the concurrence of the Treasury) concerning any of the following matters–

(a)   the fees to be paid to the registrar under this Act, so that they do not exceed in the case of the original registration of a limited partnership the sum of two pounds and, in any other case, the sum of [25p];

(b)   the duties or additional duties to be performed by the registrar for the purposes of this Act;

(c)   the performance by assistant registrars and other officers of acts by this Act required to be done by the registrar;

(d)   the forms to be used for the purposes of this Act;

(e)   generally, the conduct and regulation of legislation under this Act and any matters incidental thereto.

Appendix 3: Forms LP5 and LP6

(Registration fee £2)

LIMITED PARTNERSHIPS ACT 1907

Application for Registration of a Limited Partnership and Statement of particulars
and of the amounts contributed (in cash or otherwise) by the Limited Partners

(Pursuant to section 8 of the Limited Partnerships Act 1907)

Name of firm or partnership _____

We, the undersigned, being the partners of the above-named firm, hereby apply for registration as a limited partnership and for that
purpose supply the following particulars:

The general nature of the business

The principal place of business	The term, if any, for which the partnership is entered into

If no definite term, the conditions of existence of the partnership

Date of commencement

The partnership is limited and the full name and address of each of the partners are as follows:

General partners

Limited partners	Amounts Contributed (1)
TOTAL	

Signatures of all the partners

Date _____

Presented by: Presentor's reference:

Notes
(i)   State amount contributed by each limited partner, and whether paid in cash, or how otherwise.

Notes

The address for companies registered in England and Wales or Wales is :-

The Registrar of Companies
Companies House
Crown Way
Cardiff
CF4 3UZ

or, for companies registered in Scotland :-

The Registrar of Companies
Companies House
37 Castle Terrace
Edinburgh
EH1 2EB

Limited Partnership Act 1907

CHFP000

Statement specifying the nature of a change in the Limited Partnership and Statement of increase in the amount contributed (in cash or otherwise) by Limited Partners.

(Pursuant to section 9 of the Limited Partnerships Act 1907 and section 47 of the Finance Act 1973)

Registration No. _____

Name of firm or partnership _____

Notice is hereby given that the changes specified below have occurred in this limited partnership:

(Please see notes overleaf)

a.	The firms name Previous Name	New name
b.	General nature of the business Business previously carried on	Business now carried on
c.	Principal place of business Previous place of business	New place of business
d.	Change in the partners or the name of a partner (see Note 1)	
e.	Term of character of the partnership (see Note 2) Previous term	New term
f.	Change in the sum contributed by a limited partner (see Note 3) (particulars of any increase in capital contributions must be provided at (h) overleaf).	
g.	Change in the liability of any partner by reason of his becoming a limited instead of a general partner or vice versa.	

h. Statement of increase in capital contributions		
Name of Limited Partners	Increase or additional sum now contributed (if otherwise than in cash, that fact, with particulars, must be stated)	Total amount contributed (if otherwise than in cash, that fact, with particulars, must be stated)

Signature of firms _____ Date _____

Presented by: Presentor's reference:

NOTES

1. Changes brought about by death, by transfer of interests, by increase in the number of partners, or by change of name of any partner, must be notified here.

2. If there is, or was, no definite term, then state against 'previous term' the conditions under which the partnership was constituted and against any 'new term' the conditions under which it is now constituted.

3. Any variation in the sum contributed by any limited partner must be stated at f. overleaf. A statement of any increase in the amount of the partnership capital, whether arising from increase of contributions, or from introduction of fresh partners must also be stated at h. above.

4. Each change must be entered in the proper section a., b., c., d., e., f., g., or h., as the case may be. Provision is made in this form for notifying all the changes required by the Act to be notified, but it will frequently happen that only one item of change has to be notified. In any such case, the word 'Nil' should be inserted in the other sections.

5. The statement must be signed at the end by the firm, and delivered for registration within seven days of the changes taking place.

Appendix 4: Sample Partnership Agreement

This sample agreement is for illustrative purposes only. It is not intended to form the basis of a partnership agreement for a particular client and should not be used as such.

Where appropriate, clauses have been cross referenced to relevant sections in Chapters of this book.

This Deed of Partnership is made the 1st day of July 1998

Between

Adam Brown of 12 Herring St, Nottingham

Caroline Duke of 'Whitewalls', Talbot Lane, Nottingham

and

Ernest Farnon of 27a Pelton St, Derby

Whereas:

The parties to this Deed (the 'Partners') wish to carry on business together in partnership (the 'Partnership') under this Deed from 1 July 1999 in substitution for any previous Deed or agreement between them

1   Interpretation

1.1   In this Deed, the following words and expressions shall have the following meaning:

the 'Partnership Accountants'	Messrs Jones & Jones of 31 Stoney St, Leicester or such other firm of accountants appointed by the Partnership from time to time

'Accounting Date'	31 March in each year or such other date as the Partners may agree in writing
the 'Partnership Solicitors'	Messrs Bloggs & Bloggs of 97 Fetter St, Loughborough or such other firm of solicitors appointed by the Partnership from time to time
the 'Partnership Bank'	a bank at which the Partnership account or accounts are held
the 'Partnership Account'	an account in the name of the Partnership held at the Partnership Bank
the 'Mediator'	a person appointed by the Partnership to act as mediator in a dispute between all or any of the Partners.

1.2   In this Deed, the masculine shall include the feminine and the singular shall include the plural.

2   Business of the Partnership

The Partners are in the business of hairdressers and barbers.

3   Name of the Partnership

The name of the Partnership is 'Hair Today, Gone Tomorrow'.

[See 3.3 in Chapter 3.]

4   Place of business

The principal place of business of the Partnership is 131–33 Marshall Green Road, Nottingham.

5   Duration and dissolution

5.1   The Partnership is to continue until such time as the Partners unanimously agree that it should be dissolved and record that agreement in writing.

5.2   The death or bankruptcy of any partner shall not dissolve the Partnership.

5.3   All other partners (the 'Continuing Partners') shall have the option to purchase the share of the partner who has died or become bankrupt (the 'Former Partner').

5.3.1   If the option in 5.3 is exercised, the Continuing Partners must pay to the executors or the trustee in bankruptcy of the Former Partner (as appropriate), within three months of the notification of the death or bankruptcy to any one of the Continuing Partners, the share to which the Former Partner would have been entitled. This share is to be ascertained by reference to Clause 15.3 of this Deed which, for this purpose, shall be read as if the words 'Former Partner' were substituted for the words 'Retiring Partner'.

5.3.2   If the Continuing Partners do not exercise the option to purchase, the share of the Former Partner may be assigned to a third party or, subject to the consent of the Continuing Partners, such consent not to be unreasonably withheld, to a new partner.

[See 1.7 in Chapter 1, 5.4 in Chapter 5 and 8.1 in Chapter 8.]

6   Management and decision making

6.1   All of the Partners shall be entitled to participate in the management of the Partnership business.

6.2   A meeting of all of the Partners able to attend shall be held on the last weekday of each month (or earlier in each month if all Partners so agree). Additional meetings may be called by any partner on at least three days' notice, except in cases of emergency when shorter notice (of not less than three hours) may be given. Minutes shall be taken of each meeting and shall be approved and signed by the partners attending the next meeting. The quorum for all meetings shall be two partners. Any partner may appoint another partner as his proxy for the purpose of voting at a meeting.

6.3   Subject to the provisions of this Deed, decisions may be taken only by a majority in number of the Partners with the exception of decisions specified in Clauses 6.3.1–6.3.3 inclusive of this Deed.

6.3.1   Decisions involving expenditure of less than £100 sterling may be taken by any partner acting alone.

6.3.2   The borrowing or lending of any sum in excess of £500 may only be taken by all Partners acting unanimously.

6.3.3   Any change in the nature of the Partnership business, specified in Clause 2 of this Deed, or the admission of a new partner or the appointment or dismissal of an employee shall only be valid if all Partners have agreed to it and have recorded that agreement in writing.

[See 4.3 in Chapter 4.]

7   Duties

7.1.   Each partner will carry out his duties and obligations under this Deed with the utmost good faith and honesty.

7.2.   Each partner must account for any benefit derived directly or indirectly from the use of the Partnership name, connection or assets, unless such use has been expressly approved in writing by all other partners.

7.3   No partner may carry on a business which competes directly or indirectly with the Partnership business.

7.4   The breach of any of the duties specified in Clauses 7.1–7.3 inclusive of this Deed shall constitute a ground for expulsion under Clause 16 of this Deed.

[See 4.1 and 4.2 in Chapter 4.]

8   Time devoted to business

8.1   Each partner shall devote his full time and attention to the Partnership business. With the exception of periods of holiday specified in Clause 8.2 and absence specified in Clause 8.3, this shall include at least 35 hours per week in aggregate.

8.2   The holiday entitlement of each partner is 25 days in each calendar year, and *pro rata* for any calendar year in which a partner is admitted to, or retires from, the partnership. Such entitlement is to be taken at such times as the Partners may agree, such agreement not to be unreasonably withheld, but provided that at least two of the partners will remain available to attend to the Partnership business.

8.3   Where a partner is absent by reason of personal ill health or injury, or other personal circumstances, he shall notify the other partners as soon as reasonably practicable and, in any event, during the first working day of such absence. Where the absence extends for more than three consecutive working days or for more than five days in any 30 day period, that partner shall provide sufficient evidence in writing from a third party who is not related by birth or marriage to him of the reason for the absence.

8.4   Absences of more than 30 days in aggregate, and any unexplained absences of more than two days in aggregate (excluding holiday entitlement pursuant to Clause 8.2 of this Deed) in any 12 month period shall constitute grounds for expulsion as specified in Clause 16 of this Deed.

9   Restrictions

9.1   Upon the retirement of any partner pursuant to Clause 15 of this Deed or the expulsion of any Partner pursuant to Clause 16 of this Deed, that partner shall not, for a six month period, solicit work from any of the existing clients of the Partnership and/or set up a competing business within a one mile radius of the Partnership place of business.

9.2   A partner who has retired or been expelled shall not, at any time thereafter, represent himself to be a partner in the Partnership.

[See 5.4.2 and 5.5 in Chapter 5.]

10   Indemnity

The Partners shall indemnify each partner in respect of expenditure necessarily incurred in the ordinary course of the Partnership business or in the preservation of the Partnership property.

[See 5.4.2 in Chapter 5.]

11   Profits and losses

The net profits and losses of income of the Partnership for each Accounting Period shall be shared among the Partners in the ratio of one-half to Adam Brown, one-quarter to Caroline Duke and one-quarter to Ernest Farnon.

[See 4.4 in Chapter 4.]

12   Drawings

12.1   Each partner may draw from the Partnership income account for his own use a maximum of £1,000 in each calendar month.

12.2   If, at the end of the Accounting Period, the total drawings of any partner for that Accounting Period exceed that Partner's share of the profits for that Accounting Period, he shall repay the excess within a period to be notified to him by the other partners, such period to be not less than one month from the date of notification.

[See 4.4. in Chapter 4.]

13   Keeping of books.

The Partnership books and accounts, including a copy of this Deed, shall be open to inspection by any partner or his agent during normal working hours on the giving of 24 hours' notice by that partner to the other partners.

14   Dispute resolution

In the event of any dispute between the Partners which cannot be resolved by them, the Partners agree to try to resolve the dispute through mediation. If the Partners cannot agree on the appointment of a Mediator, a Mediator is to be appointed by CEDR and the fees be met equally by all of the Partners. The Mediator is to have the power to inspect any of the Partnership books or accounts and to convene meetings with the Partners. Any agreement reached by the Partners through the Mediator is to be legally binding.

[See 7.1 and 7.2 in Chapter 7.]

15   Retirement

15.1   Any partner may retire from the Partnership at any time by giving at least three months' notice in writing to all other partners (the 'Continuing Partners') that he (the 'Retiring Partner') wishes to retire.

15.2   The Continuing Partners shall have the option to purchase the share of the Retiring Partner.

15.2.1   If this option is exercised, the Continuing Partners must pay to the Retiring Partner the share to which he is entitled under Clause 15.3 of this Deed within three months of the retirement.

15.2.2   If the Continuing Partners do not exercise the option to purchase, the Retiring Partner may assign his share to a third party or, subject to the consent of the Continuing Partners, such consent not to be unreasonably withheld, to a new partner.

15.3   The share to which the Retiring Partner is entitled shall be ascertained by reference to his original capital contribution as specified in Clause 17 of this Deed, together with his share of any undrawn profits according to Clause 11 of this Deed, and his share of any capital profits in the same proportion as his capital contribution bore to the total original capital of the Partnership as specified in Clause 17 of this Deed.

15.4   The Retiring Partner is to co-operate as required by the Continuing Partners in notifying clients and suppliers of the Partnership of his retirement.

[See 5.4.2 in Chapter 5.]

16   Expulsion

16.1   Any partner may be expelled if the other partners acting unanimously consider that he (the 'Expelled Partner') has been guilty of breaches of this Deed, financial fraud or misconduct relating to the Partnership business, or any other conduct prejudicial to the Partnership business, or has become bankrupt or gone into liquidation or is suffering from permanent physical incapacity or mental incapacity, and that this justifies expulsion.

16.2   Subject to Clause 16.4 of this Deed, the partner whose expulsion is sought must be given notice in writing of the conduct giving rise to the expulsion at least 72 hours prior to any expulsion and must be given the opportunity to explain in writing or orally to the other partners his position before a final vote on expulsion is taken. The partner may be suspended from the Partnership between the giving of notice and the final vote and, during the period of suspension, may not participate in management of the Partnership or any other Partnership business.

16.3   If, within 72 hours of notice being provided to a partner under Clause 16.2 of this Deed, that partner has not provided any explanation of his conduct, or such explanation has failed to satisfy the other partners that the grounds listed in Clause 16.1 of this Deed do not apply, or that they do not justify expulsion, a vote on the expulsion shall be taken. The expulsion shall only be carried out if all partners other than the partner to be expelled vote in favour in person or by proxy.

16.4 The procedure provided for in Clause 16.2 of this Deed shall not apply where a partner is guilty of gross misconduct (including, but not limited to, financial misconduct relating to the Partnership business, wilful breach or persistent breaches of this Deed and any other misconduct directly affecting the Partnership business or clients of the Partnership). In such cases, the partner may be expelled summarily by the other partners pursuant to Clause 16.1 of this Deed.

16.5 In the event that a partner is expelled, Clauses 15.2 to 15.4 inclusive of this Deed shall apply and shall be read as if the words 'Expelled Partner' were substituted for the words 'Retiring Partner'.

[See 7.4 in Chapter 7.]

17 Capital

17.1 The Partnership is commenced with a total capital of £10,000 of which:

£5,000 has been contributed by Adam Brown in the form of £1,000 cash and £4,000 being the value of the lease of the premises at 131–33 Marshall Green Road, Nottingham assigned to the Partnership by the said Adam Brown;

£3,000 has been contributed by Caroline Duke in the form of £2,000 cash and £1,000 worth of stock-in-trade; and

£2,000 has been contributed by Ernest Farnon in the form of £2,000 cash.

17.2 This capital, together with the profits and losses relating to such capital (including partnership property), shall belong to the Partners in the proportions in which it has been contributed by them.

17.3 Further contributions of capital shall be made as required from time to time by agreement of a majority in number of the Partners.

[See 4.4 in Chapter 4.]

18   Property

18.1   All the vehicles, furniture, safes, professional and computer equipment, intellectual property rights, confidential information (whether written or stored in electronic form) and all other property in or about the Partnership premises and used or acquired for the purposes of the Partnership business shall belong to the Partners jointly in the proportions in which the capital is shared.

18.2   Partnership property is to be held and applied solely for the purposes of the Partnership business.

[See 3.4 in Chapter 3.]

19   Insurance

The Partners shall at all times ensure that adequate insurance is maintained in respect of all Partnership property and liabilities of the Partnership.

20   Goodwill

20.1   No payment is to be made on account of goodwill to any partner save on dissolution.

20.2   The goodwill of this Partnership on dissolution is to be calculated by the Partnership Accountants according to its book value.

[See 3.4.6 in Chapter 3.]

21   Bank details

21.1   No withdrawal from the Partnership Account of more than £100 in cash may be made without the prior agreement of at least two of the Partners.

21.2   Any cheque drawn on the Partnership Account must be signed by two of the Partners.

22   Accounting details

22.1   A copy of the Partnership Accounts for all years shall be kept at the Partnership premises and shall be available for inspection by any of the Partners during normal working hours.

22.2   A copy of the Partnership Accounts for each year shall be given to each of the Partners within one month of the Accounting Date. The Partnership Accounts shall be approved at the first Partnership meeting held pursuant to Clause 6.2 of this Deed after all of the Partners have received a copy of the Partnership Accounts.

23   Amending the agreement

23.1   This Deed shall be amended only by the written consent of all Partners.

23.2   A copy of any amendments to this Deed shall be provided to each Partner and attached to the copy of this Deed kept at the Partnership premises and to the copy of this Deed held by the Partnership Solicitors within one month of the amendment being made pursuant to Clause 23.1 of this Deed.

[See 3.2 in Chapter 3.]

24   Winding up and insolvency

A petition for a partnership voluntary arrangement or administration order may only be made by a majority in number of the Partners.

[See Chapter 9.]